Your 12 Step Guide to Full-Time Speaking Right Now!
*The Speakerpreneur: SECRETS SIMPLIFIED FOR BOTH BEGINNER,
INTERMEDIATE & ADVANCED SPEAKERS to Earn $5k - $25k+ Per
Engagement!*

Copyright © 2025 by COURTNEY J POINTER LEWIS

*All rights reserved. No part of this book may be reproduced or transmitted in any
form or by any means without written permission from the author.*

ISBN: 979-8-9996090-1-4

DEDICATION

Dedicated to my family who supports me endlessly through my quest to deliver the truth to those seeking freedom—whether financial, spiritual, emotional in whole.

Thank you for encouraging me to be my best, even when it's a sacrifice to you. I'm forever grateful.

With all my love,

Courtney J.

TABLE OF CONTENTS

INTRODUCTION 1

THE 12 STEP PROCESS TO FULL-TIME SPEAKERPRENEURSHIP 14

STEP 1: THE UNMOVABLE DECISION ON THE FINANCIAL GOAL 16

STEP 2: IDENTITY & INDUSTRY – CHOOSE THE SERVICE "WORLD" YOU'RE CALLED TO 26

STEP 3: YOUR SPEAKER IDENTITY – CLAIMING A TITLE THE WORLD UNDERSTANDS 38

STEP 4: AVATAR WORK – KNOWING WHO YOU'RE CALLED TO SERVE DEEPLY 50

STEP 5: OFFER – DESIGNING A TANGIBLE, SALIVATING SOLUTION 68

STEP 6: CLEAR MESSAGE – WHAT YOU STAND FOR AND HOW IT ALIGNS WITH YOUR OFFER 80

STEP 7: BRAND IDENTITY – BECOMING THE GO-TO VOICE & VISION IN YOUR SPACE 89

STEP 8: PRODUCT CREATION – BUILDING YOUR WEALTH LADDER 97

STEP 9: THE SIGNATURE SPEECH – SHARING YOUR STORY, SHIFTING THE ROOM 110

STEP 10: TRAFFIC & LEAD MAGNETS – BRINGING PEOPLE INTO YOUR WORLD 120

STEP 11: SALES PROCESS – GUIDING YOUR AUDIENCE TO SAY YES WITH CONFIDENCE 132

STEP 12: BACKEND SYSTEMS – DELIVERING WITH EXCELLENCE AND EASE 156

ABOUT THE AUTHOR 171

INTRODUCTION

This isn't necessarily a book per se...

It's more like the ultimate, full-fledged guide to exploding your speaking career quickly, mixed with multiple thought-provoking speaking business sessions on paper.

Don't be surprised if you get emotional... or if you realize the steps go way deeper than you initially thought. This guide will challenge you to lay every element/part of your speaking business... and even your other ventures — out in the open...

Afterward, you'll find yourself mesmerized, standing before answers you didn't know were already within you...

Ready to shape them into a marvelous, powerful, personalized system and structure designed solely by you with help from myself and the Lord.

Have you ever wanted to take success into your own hands so badly that it almost hurt?

Well... whether you're ready or not, you've started that journey today, simply by reading and engaging with this guide.

But before we go any further, let me take you back real quick... so you can understand a bit about my past and how what I'm revealing in this guide changed everything for me.

It's important to start by saying this: I come from a military and West Indian background.

If you know, you know... there was no tolerance for low performance with that type of background.

That's just how I was raised...

"Work hard and put family first." Even then, I always knew I wanted to be a business owner.

This picture right here — one of my first businesses: ironing clothes in the back yard.

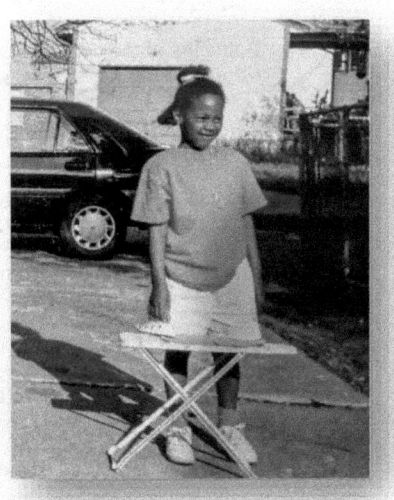

As you can see it made no sense lol... No plug. No heat = No results. SMH. DUH.

But my grandparents still cheered me on and said, "Great job!"

And I love them for that, because in that moment, I felt so seen and loved.

They even doubled down on it with that picture lol.

Was that affirmation needed? Absolutely. Especially coming from a background where my mother — too young and too overwhelmed to care for me — left me.

I was raised by my grandparents.
That love from them? I needed it to survive... literally.

But did it also play a role in the detriment of how I later approached business? Yes... yes, it did.

To some, this may seem harmless...
But for me, it created a pattern.

I began to see business through a lens of:
Acceptance = A good job, instead of:

A good job = The reward of a targeted outcome being achieved.
And let's be honest... the traits of every hyper-successful business owner (including speakerpreneurs like us) are clear:

- Hitting consistent, measurable goals in both sales and impact.

- Staying committed through the pivots, even when things get hard.

- Doing the same high-level routines again and again, without skipping a beat... even when you're over it.

I didn't understand it at the time, but I wasn't prepared for that level of discipline... none of it.

I had been conditioned to run away from places and people that "didn't want me", straight into the arms of anything or anyone that made me feel safe.

I was ready to make big moves with no plan and no mentor... and then cry when the outcome obviously didn't yield success.

This was not the trait of a disciplined business owner.....

That's not the mindset of a wounded army leader who fights to the end even in chaos, to help bring home victory.

That was the trait of a wounded soldier that decided the pain was too great even if it put the whole squad at risk. The one who says "Leave me here, I've had enough."

That was my daily mental operating system. My silent SOP.

And I didn't even know it. It needed healing. It needed reframing.

We love to quote "Train up a child in the way he should go..."

But we forget... that goes both ways. For better or worse.

I loved business, but I was one of those people that was working multiple six figure corporate jobs, not one... multiple.

Telling myself, "I'm doing this so I can invest in my business."

... But all the while, God kept telling me (and I know some of you all are going through this right now)...

"Courtney, I need you to build the company that I called you to build. The healing, the life everything you desire and need is wrapped up in that."

And I said, "I got it, God. I'm building it. I promise."

But that was the problem. "I" was building instead of "We". I had to be honest...

I was still showing favoritism to my employment rather than strategically learning, pushing & elevating the business God told me to build at rapid speed like my job couldn't one day vanish. I thought I was safe... "job safety".

The same kind of safety I learned to cling to in childhood. The same safety, I would eventually be fired from.

Yes, I was meant to show up and do my job well. But the level of discipline I gave to that job?

That should've just as aggressively been distributed into my calling.

If your business success is tied to your speaking career, please let this be a wake-up call.

Don't delay what God has told you to do. Stop saying, "Just one more year, God," whether you realize you're saying it or not. If you're already pursuing your speaking career, stop only telling stories - start garnering the respect your years of training & influence at your job is worth... more on this later...

The point is...
You *can* do both... *But* I didn't then.

And eventually, my dreams shattered.

My health hit rapid declines. The hospital became a frequent destination due to high stress levels. I'd neglected the person who held the purpose... me.

You know as well as I do... No matter how good you are at helping others succeed... that dedication won't carry you forever if you're not answering your own divine assignment.

Things got even worse real fast. Those multiple six-figure jobs? Gone... and suddenly...

I was homeless.

I remember sitting in a U-Haul truck... full of shame. I had been living there for a few weeks.

And unfortunately, the suppression gift my trauma usually activated...

Yeah... it wasn't kicking in this time.

I glanced over at my husband, asleep beside me.

He was physically ill and struggling to breathe from an autoimmune issue he had and now the fumes from the truck were deeply affecting his body, his sleep interrupted by tremors.

I felt the tears well up...

But then... I got angry.

Furious at the life I helped create.

There was power in that anger... because I was fed up with being the same.

The same woman.

In the same situation.

With the same achievements...
Even when I thought I was doing something different.

Or was I?

I was confused.

I said, "God, what is this crap that I'm in right now?"

I felt embarrassed. Misunderstood. Tired physically...

And mentally sick.

I felt like an imposter. A straight up fraud.

Speaking affirmations of change yet living in a literal pit.

At that moment, I was tempted to question my entire life... "Why am I even living?"

You see, I think a lot of people hear these types of thoughts, these emotions, these questions... as weaknesses.

But the truth?

Anyone who has ever done anything great... anyone who's achieved success beyond the norm in any field, knows these questions...

They carry atomic power.

The kind of power that unlocks secrets.

Secrets that unlock open up a world far beyond what someone who only sees themselves as "just human" could ever tap into.

I firmly believe we were never designed to function in only this physical realm... in this little room some folks have locked themselves into.

And even for those who don't believe in Jesus... or in God...

Even then — the signs are still all around us.

It's evident...

No... infallibly clear...

That there is something far beyond us.

A power that cannot be explained.

A power that can't be contained.

And once you tap into it?

It courses through every blood vessel, every vein, every part of your human existence and causes you to do things that can only be described as...

Supernatural.

Gaining hundreds of thousands — even millions of dollars — isn't difficult when you understand the supernatural power within you.

In fact, it actually becomes quite minute... and honestly, one of the easiest things you can do is obtain money.

And while yes, we are supernatural beings (and as we get to know each other more you'll definitely hear me talk about this a lot) ...

There are still technical steps involved in cashing in on the God-given abilities within you, the ones designed to help you produce cash here on earth.

I personally found my way out of that U-Haul truck and into a life of financial and mental independence... a level of freedom that can only be explained through the steps and lessons I'm about to share with you in this guide...

and the volumes to come.

These lessons, the ones I've gained over my 15-year speaking and business journey, have taken me from merely existing to actually living.

They've positioned me for financial freedom as a speaker and entrepreneur...

And now... I'm passing them on to you.

Understand this: the principles I'm giving you are very, very simple.

Don't underestimate them because of that.

Truth lies in simplicity. Truth lies in principle.

I often teach people to look for what I call the "truth root" — the basic principle at the heart of every subject — because when you find that, you will always have success.

When you master simplicity, and when you master truth... your life, your bank account, and everything else that matters becomes extravagant.

People overcomplicate life way too much...

So of course, people overcomplicate speaking, services, and products too.

As you read through this guide, I'm going to give you the foundation — the base — of everything you need to build your own version of success.

And honestly?

The smallest thing this guide will do for you... is help you become financially independent through speakerpreneurship.
This guide will change your life... your children's lives...

and generations to come, especially in the area of financial freedom and independence through speaking, business, and money ethics.

Financial independence and diversifying income isn't just a desire, it's a necessity for safety here on earth.

I also believe it's a spiritual necessity.

In order for us to bring the Kingdom to earth... we must be able to finance it. Financial dependence can be a major distraction.

And when systems fail, or the government has its own plans, we must be able to finance and find safety within our own wealth system.

Now, some people will tell you to quit your job in order to be a full-time speaker.

That's not what this book is about.

I believe you must listen to your inner voice to determine what your path looks like.

And if you choose to lay your job down everything you need is here to support it.

Whether you remain employed and build your independent speaking source on the side, or you go full-time into speaking the key is this:

A financially independent <u>mindset</u> and diversified income opens the door to a new level of safety.

As you review these steps, go deeper... remember don't just read with your natural eyes and ears.

Engage with your spiritual senses.
Let this guide speak to more than just your mind... let it speak to your spirit.

I've practiced these very steps for over 15 years — consistently.

They've helped me not only build a full-time speaking career, but build new businesses, refine existing ones, and support others in scaling their own visions with speed and integrity.

This guide is about speed, but it's also about foundation and ethics in your speaking career.

And yes... we will go deep.

It took me nearly a decade of time and financial investments to discover the simplicity of these steps.

You're receiving them in about five minutes of check out...

Oh, the joys of sowing seeds. Amen.

Let me remind you... you are not "trying" to create finances on this earth...

You are not "trying" to become rich.

The finances have already been placed within you...

You have already been created in financial abundance.

So, let's begin the process of pulling more out of you.

Every step in this guide must be studied deeply...

Every resource in this volume and the ones to come deserves your full attention.

And listen — no need to be overwhelmed... don't get discouraged... if something doesn't click right away.

Keep studying. Keep leaning in.

Revelation will hit you like a ton of bricks, just like it did for me and for so many others who applied these principles.

Don't wait for perfection to start momentum.

Don't wait. Start now. Start with what you have.
Write on every page.

Because what's in you is already enough to move.

Your momentum will bring understanding… more clarity… and more results.

You'll be required to take quiet reflection time at the end of each session and journal what the Lord is leading you to do.

Then?

Create an action plan.

Don't wait.

Start implementing immediately… even if it's one small step.

You already know your life is a gift, a divine setup for advancement.

You already know you possess incredible power.

Now it's time to move in it.

You know God gave you the power to receive wealth
on this Earth. (Duet 8:18)

The question is always…
has always been…
and will always be…

What more are you going to do with it?

What are you truly willing to receive from it?

Before we dive into the deep, let's crash course into a few highly valuable points, so we can set the stage for you to truly gather the fullness of the 12 steps we'll discuss.

K.I.S.S.

We had an old mentor who taught us this acronym...

It stands for: **"Keep it simple, stupid."**

I've sat under some of the best.

But only those who could break down the simplicity of success ever really got my attention.

No bull crap.

That's always been my motto.

You can be entertaining, of course…

but give me the truth, with speed.

I can handle it.

I'm sure you're probably a bit like me.

I like simple, quick things and I want you to keep it simple & quick too.

Because making money through your speaking and entrepreneurial endeavors isn't complicated.

I'm married.

I'm a little "extra."

I've got a big family.

Trust me… the rest of my life is extravagant and complicated enough. LOL.

In fact, it's my firm belief

that those who create tension around making money…

those who see money-making as difficult & slow…

will always have a hard time receiving the amount they desire.

Let's talk facts for a moment:

A study from the University of Wisconsin–Madison found that individuals who believed in the importance of financial independence tended to have higher actual incomes.

Why?

Because their belief was the fuel.

It motivated them to earn more.

It's another confirmation of the science of neuroplasticity... the brain adapts to repeated thoughts.

So, when someone frequently thinks, "Making money is hard," those thoughts create strong neural pathways.

The brain begins to process every financial opportunity as a threat or a struggle.

Those thought patterns become subconscious default settings... especially when new ideas, new risks, or new goals show up...like starting a business, expanding your reach, or negotiating higher pay.

Result: Individuals may unconsciously sabotage potential financial progress due to internalized mental resistance. I'm mentioning this because it will be imperative that through this process you stretch your mind to new levels of wealth. We will come back to this in a few.

Let's move forward and bring something else important to the table: Glossophobia — the anxiety disorder associated with a fear of public speaking.

It's a type of social anxiety where individuals feel intense fear just thinking about speaking in front of others.

In fact, approximately 75% to 77% of the population experience some level of fear or anxiety when it comes to public speaking.

Which means...

You're in the 25%.

Your ability to step on stage, speak with power, and deliver a message... that's a superpower.

It's a rare gift.

And rare gifts...

Bring rare wealth.

Now that you know this...

Now that you know I don't sugarcoat anything...

I'm going to make a bold statement:

No speaker who has an entrepreneurial mind should ever be under six figures a year.

Period.

It shouldn't even be humanly possible.

If they are, there are only a few possible reasons:

- Mindset issues (including focus & bad time management)
- Spiritual money blocks
- Lack of mentorship

That's where this guide comes in.

That's where I come in.

Because the truth is… the gift of speaking isn't as common as most people think.

And if only 25% - 30% of people can do it with clarity and confidence, then yes… it comes with privilege.

It comes with benefits.

But here's the problem…

Most speakers and entrepreneurs struggle financially because they don't treat speaking as a business.

They see it as a story, a testimony, a passion, or a powerful word only… but not a profit-producing system.

They treat it like a hobby… instead of the business vehicle it's meant to be.

Sadly, this is the same issue many entrepreneurs face across the board…

I don't know exactly when it got twisted.

But I'm guessing it's a trick of the evil one.

Maybe it ties back to Revelation 13:16–17, where we see a warning about economic control… a "beast system" governed by allegiance to darkness.

That passage illustrates a satanic economic structure, one where access to money and resources is manipulated and restricted.

It reminds us:

Wealth can be spiritually influenced.

Satan absolutely desires control over how people earn and spend.

Fast forward to today — culture, media, even parts of business culture — have been infiltrated.

There's a constant push to worship money, live in fear of lack, or operate in greed.

It's often coded in the language we use: branding, lyrics, affirmations — even well-meaning ones — that subtly replace God's truth with deception.

And yet, the Word is clear.

Ecclesiastes 10:19 says, "Money answereth all things." In the material world, money is a tool.

It is often received through the service of your gifts.
So let me say this loud and clear.
Highlight it. Circle it. Let it hit you:

Your money is here **NOW** & ready to be withdrawn!

If you've ever been exposed to my teachings, or even if this is your first time…

You'll hear me reference what I call the mom and dad of marketing: Offer and Traffic.

Then we add these other essentials: Sales and Service Delivery.

These four — Offer, Traffic, Sales, and Service Delivery — form the basic structure you must master if you want to even touch six figures & beyond consistently as a full-time speaker.

And yes, this applies directly to your speaking business.

Because your speaking business is… a BUSINESS.

Your speaking business is also YOU.

It's your voice.

It's your message.

It's how you communicate that message to the world.

Which means…

You take your speaking business everywhere you go.

You could be pitching in the grocery store.

Presenting in a coffee shop…

Or sharing your story with just one person who needs it… and that one could open a $100K+ speaking contract door.

I talk about this in one of my webinars — how in the docu depiction "WeCrashed", Adam Neumann, founder of WeWork, literally saved his company from millions in debt…

The major key? Just one speaking engagement, with one person in mind…who turned around and gave him $4.4 billion.

If we continue to hold onto the toxic, limited belief that "speaking" only happens on physical stages to large crowds and packed events...

Then we not only cap our income potential...
we disconnect from the truth: that we are entrepreneurs first, not just speakers

In essence, we must expand our thinking around what it truly means to be a speaker... or an entrepreneur.

Because we are not just one or the other.

We are both.

We are Speakerpreneurs.

And as we step into the 12 steps on the next page, I want you to understand something clearly:

These are the EXACT steps I teach inside my private trainings...

the same steps that have helped thousands of speakerpreneurs achieve financial independence and true freedom.

These steps are the foundation of everything I teach.

The only difference?

In my private containers, I coach clients one-on-one or more closely through each piece.

And many of them?

All over the globe, different ages, ethnic groups and family dynamics...

They're earning at least $100K every 90 days, at minimum.

So, this system works.

But today?

This is the first time I'm making all of it public.

I'm honored to sow this seed into the world - by planting it in you.

God said the time is now.

And I know you're ready.

So, let's get it.

THE 12 STEP PROCESS TO FULL-TIME SPEAKERPRENEURSHIP

Welcome to the Speakerpreneur Pyramid, your visual at-a-glance guide.

This chart outlines a basic order from the ground up, with light notes next to each section to add to your guided journey.

You'll find powerful reflection questions to consider as you move through this full guide...

Don't rush, let each layer unfold.

THE 12 STEP SPEAKERPRENEUR PYRAMID

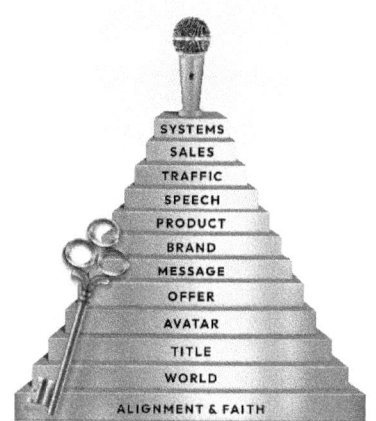

Here are a few brief condensed notes from each section that we will cover in this guide.

1. Faith – Things to consider: an unmovable decision on your financial goal; a clear vision of what you want and what you are calling into existence.

2. What "world" are you in? Make a decision about the overall person or industry you feel called to serve — e.g., "mothers," "fathers," "troubled teens," "therapy," "dentistry," "fitness," "diabetes."

3. What is your clear title description? Choose a title the world understands at large.

4. Who is your ideal avatar? List their good and bad traits. What are they Googling that fits your title or service?

5. Offer – What is the tangible, salivating solution you provide, and how will you deliver it?

6. Clear Message – What do you stand for as a person and company, and how does that relate to your offer?

7. Brand – When your potential client sees you and your service, what do they associate you with? What do they see you as? What does it look like you provide? What do you stand for? Do they feel safe?

8. Product Creation Examples –

- Low ticket = book, PDF, webinar

- Mid ticket = course or group coaching

- High ticket = 1-on-1 consulting, high-ticket workshops or group consulting, corporate training and speaking contracts, keynote speaking

9. Speech – Write your speech using your chosen story that matches your offer and correlates with your avatar.

10. Traffic Source & Lead Magnets – Decide what types of paid and organic traffic sources you will use to bring people to your brand, products, and services.

11. Sales Process – Decide how you will guide people through the funnel to buy each service. Consider sales calls, independent sales carts, etc.

12. Backend Systems – Tech and service delivery process: how you will provide what has been sold and how you will store client information.

As I mentioned, these are simple yet profound. As you master each of these steps, you will find yourself closer to and more advanced in the seat of full-time speakerpreneurship.

Now, let's dive into Step 1.

STEP 1: THE UNMOVABLE DECISION ON THE FINANCIAL GOAL

Introduction: Your Mindset is the Foundation

Every speakerpreneur's journey begins with one thing: belief.

Not just any belief, but an unmovable, unshakable, unapologetically bold decision to achieve a specific financial goal.

This is the cornerstone of your full-time speaking career.

This kind of belief isn't wishful thinking.

It's a deliberate, empowered choice to align your thoughts, emotions, and actions with the financial future you see for yourself.

If you felt a little icky or uncomfortable reading that, it's likely because your mindset around money and financial goals has been tainted somewhere along the way.

That, my friend, is what I call a toxic money mindset.

People with this issue often see money as something outside of what it truly is... a part of your overall health and well-being.

You don't reach your financial goals by accident.

You didn't get your job by accident either.

So right now, take a moment to cleanse any old, limiting beliefs around money.

Say this quickly and confidently:

"Money is a part of my overall health. There's nothing icky about it. In fact, I handle financial abundance and money very well. I control massive amounts of money and can use it as I desire.

Money does not control me. Making money runs through my DNA. I am abundant in every area of life. Therefore, no amount of money or any other abundance on this Earth is foreign to me.

Abundance is normal. Massive amounts of money are normal, and they flow to and through me naturally through my gifts. My full-time speaking career is a done deal."

Here's a tip I like to share: Give yourself a minimum achievement goal, not a maximum goal, because you are limitless.

The highest level you can even imagine is only the amount your faith can hold.

The lowest level you're willing to accept? That might be the maximum your body, mind, or current situation can physically handle right now.

That lowest cap is your starting point. From there, you break through to your highest level of faith — and then beyond what you ever dreamed possible.

For example, say this:

"The minimum amount of money I've ever made is **[insert your lowest cap]**. I immediately graduated to **[insert the highest level you can confidently say out loud]** so I can be **[insert your deeper reason for accepting this abundance, like 'a pillar of the abundance God represents on this earth for my community']**."

Be honest with yourself. Update your lowest goal when you achieve it and raise your highest goal as your faith grows.

Get specific about these two numbers.

You might want to match your current job income this year and make a minimum of $100K annually on your own. That's your base goal.

Then you might also want to make $5,000,000 annually within the next 5 years.

As you write these down, start shifting your mindset from "what I want" to "I've made".

Because once you set that goal in place, it's no longer just a goal… it becomes an event that has already happened supernaturally and is now moving in the earthly realm, powered by your confession and intention.

Now it's your job to align your body, soul, and spirit so it can show up fully and equally in all areas of your life.

You have become the man or woman who lives the life your words create — whether that's a certain level of luxury, high-level living, personal growth, or the inner work that fuels outer success.

You are uniquely positioned as a rich, wealthy, impactful speakerpreneur.

But this all starts with a clear vision.

This step is designed to walk you through making that vision real in your mind, so it can be made evident in your life.

Work out the steps from above and add your own personal references and reminders that ground you here…

Section 1: What Is Mindset In The Context Of Financial Independence?

We understand that mindset is everything. It's the lens through which you see your possibilities, make decisions, and create your results.

In full-time speakerpreneurship, mindset involves choosing to believe in your financial independence before you have proof.

It's standing firm even when others — including yourself — have doubts. It's taking intentional action while trusting your ability to shape reality with your thoughts and energy, tapping into your supernatural power.

Financial independence here isn't about greed; it's about health, freedom, impact, and legacy. When you set your financial goal, you're not just naming a number. You're declaring your ability to design a life that reflects your highest potential on every level. That's why you set both a minimum and maximum goal for your belief.

Faith is the substance of things hoped for, the evidence of things not seen. (Note: There is evidence — remember to look for it.) In speakerpreneurship, faith means choosing to believe in your financial independence through speaking before any audience books you, before any products sell, and before any stages are graced. It's taking strategic action while trusting in God's supernatural backing.

Section 2: Make The Unshakable Decision

You must decide.

Not hope. Not wish. Not try.

Decide.

The word trying irks me. I say, "You either do it, or you don't!"

This decision anchors your mindset. Write down your financial goal. Be specific.

Don't say, "I want to make more money." Say, "I now, at minimum, earn $500,000 per year through my speaker business by **[insert date]**."

This declaration is your mental and spiritual contract. Post it on your mirror.

Say it aloud every morning. Journal it every night. LIVE IN IT within your imagination, physically if you can, let it permeate your life and spill over.

Ask yourself: What does my life look like now that I've achieved this goal?

What parts of that can I mirror in my life today?

Soon, you'll see no difference between the world lived in your imagination and the world occupied by your body, they will be one and the same.

This isn't about hyping yourself up; it's about aligning your mindset and actions with your desired outcome.

This is what Jesus did when he spoke to the fig tree. This is what God did when He shaped the earth. This is your supernatural power to create worlds.

Reference:

Jesus & the tree — Mark 11 (NIV)

God's creation process broken out — Genesis 1 (NIV)

Section 3: Activate Belief Through Daily Practice

Belief without action is fantasy. You'll learn principles and strategies throughout this guide, but principles and strategies without belief will only burn you out.

Your belief fuels your business. Every sales page, social post, pitch, and stage performance becomes a seed when it's backed by certainty.

Here are a few daily habits to strengthen your belief:

I recommend doing these at least 2-3 times a day.

- Declarations: Speak your financial goal aloud in the present tense.

- Vision Meditation: Close your eyes and see your life as if the goal is already accomplished.

- Gratitude Practice: Feel genuine appreciation for what you have and what's coming your way.

- Prophetic Journaling: Write letters or journal entries as if your goals are already real... because they are.

Take this time to release habits that you know you need to change in order to become the best version of yourself. Add any other notes to create new ones below.

_____
_____
_____
_____
_____
_____
_____
_____
_____
_____

Section 4: Use Imagination In Your Business Strategy

Countless mindset experts and myself included agree that imagination is the most powerful creative force. In my course Supernatural Sales, I teach how to use imagination to clear toxic thoughts around money. That course is bible and science based. Science and success stories confirm this: your brain can't tell the difference between a vividly imagined reality and one you actually live.

Imagination is how you build the invisible. Remember the Tower of Babel? Even the Lord couldn't stop the building if the people were united and focused on what they imagined coming to pass.

Likewise, it's my personal revelation that when spirit, body, and soul align, nothing you imagine is impossible.

When you imagine yourself on stage, decked out in your brand colors, confidently pitching your high-ticket offer to an engaged audience and getting paid 4, 5, or 6, 7 figures or more... you're creating a mental blueprint.

Let me be clear: this is not daydreaming. This is strategic visualization.

Exercises to implement:

- Prepare a time map for how you will complete this process. You can't implement strategy or principles without making time for them. One of my old mentors always says, "What doesn't get scheduled, doesn't get done." Start by mapping out your actual daily time, then adjust it realistically based on what you can commit to.

- Create a Vision Board that includes your revenue goals, event photos, client testimonials, and luxury lifestyle desires.

- Record a visualization script in the present tense using "I am" statements and listen to it daily.

- Write a one-page journal entry from the perspective of the version of you who has already achieved these goals.

Have a few notes to jot down before moving on? Feel free to use this space.

_____

_____

_____

_____

Section 5: Co-Creating Your Future With Intention

You are the co-creator of your success. God has already promised it to you. Your mind is the command center. As you build your speaking business and any other ventures... stay tuned to inspiration, intuition, Holy Spirit guidance, and alignment.

Your financial goal isn't just for you... it's a pathway to impact, authentic expression, and an elevated life that flows out to those around you.

Exercises to implement:

- Meditate on your goals daily.

- Set clear intentions before making business decisions. Seek the Spirit within you for guidance. Ask for divine instructions before every major move.

- Practice generosity and abundance from the start... give what you can, even before the money flows.

- Pray over your financial goals regularly.

- Sow seeds of faith from day one, even when your earnings are at a minimum.

You weren't made to play small... that's a choice. You were created to prosper, influence, and thrive.

Your Notes:

_____
_____
_____
_____
_____
_____
_____
_____

Conclusion: From Decision to Manifestation

You've made the unshakable decision to pursue financial independence through speakerpreneurship with a strong, empowered mindset. You've written down your goal. You're aligned in vision and strategy. The rest of this guide will walk you through the practical steps... but without that unmovable faith, none of the strategies will work in a healthy aligned way.

Mindset is your superpower. Faith is your stance. Use it. Stand in it. Declare it boldly.

Be as specific as possible... even when visualizing your systems of achievement as they come together.

You are now a full-time speakerpreneur building wealth on purpose.

So, Let's build!

Here's some extra space to release your thoughts from what you've learned so far or what God is speaking to you.

_____
_____
_____
_____
_____
_____
_____
_____
_____
_____
_____
_____
_____
_____
_____

REFLECTION & ACTION TIME

Use this time to reflect over your notes, pray/meditate and make a plan of action from this step accordingly. Use an additional notebook if necessary, add dates and times to carry out the mission.

Goal | (Event that has Occurred in the spirit realm).

What is the specific goal or milestone you're focusing on right now?

_____

_____

_____

Steps Leading to the Goal

Break down the steps you need to take to reach this goal, one by one.

_____

_____

_____

Potential Obstacles

What might get in the way of you completing these steps?

_____

_____

_____

Support System

Who or what can help you overcome these obstacles or keep them manageable?

_____

_____

_____

STEP 2: IDENTITY & INDUSTRY – CHOOSE THE SERVICE "WORLD" YOU'RE CALLED TO

Introduction: Clarity is the Catalyst for Wealth

To build a profitable full-time business, you must first know exactly who you are and who you're meant to serve. I always say two things:

"The more you know yourself, the more money you will make… and the more you care for others, the more money you will make as well."

Knowing who you are also saves you from so much turmoil in your business. It helps you avoid building something that secretly disgusts you because you created it out of desperation—out of need, greed, insecurity, or misalignment—instead of purpose and clarity.

Your "world" is divinely chosen. It's a combination of what you're drawn to and what the Spirit of God confirms in you. And that's what leads you to clarity.

This is how you function as a full-time speakerpreneur that operates in wholeness of spirit, soul & body… Not just money.

Without clarity, your message is scattered. Your offers become confusing. And your audience won't recognize that you are the answer they've been searching for.

But when you choose your world, the specific industry or community you feel deeply called to… everything becomes magnetic.

Let's simplify this. I'm not talking about your general avatar yet. I'm talking about the broader world, the total population. This is about the industry, the bigger picture, the space in which you'll serve. We'll narrow it down to the specific person later.

Financially independent speakers don't try to speak to everyone. They own one space, one lane, one world at a time. And when they do, the world listens.

That's the key: to reach the one piece, you must first decide on the whole. The full population. The space you're called to move in. That's how I help my clients go beyond just "picking a niche."

Why? Because like you, many of us have multiple gifts and passions. So, they must be structured in worlds—industries—so we can manage them with care and in proper timing.

Start with the world, then narrow it to the people within it.

You can serve mothers as a world and later go deeper into supporting moms raising children with cleft lips.

You can serve the health food industry and later niche into plant-based meal prep for busy professionals.

This step will guide you through identifying your core industry… the broader audience you're uniquely called to serve. And as you get clearer on that, the purpose-driven niche within it will begin to emerge naturally.

Now you're stepping into your power, your passion, your precision, your purpose… and yes, your profit.

Section 1: What is Your "World"?

Your world is the space you're called to dominate as a speakerpreneur. It's the community, industry, or topic where your voice carries weight, your experience brings value, and your message sparks movement.

You can have multiple offers and streams of income within one world, we'll explore how to do that later.

This is about claiming a space where your calling and credibility collide.

Examples of "Worlds":

- Speaker World - Women, Men
- Author World – Children
- Real estate investors – All
- Corporate professionals in burnout – Women
- Stay-at-home moms - rebuilding self-worth
- Fitness entrepreneurs - Start-ups
- Nurses in leadership – Hospitals
- Women with autoimmune diseases
- Creatives navigating career pivots
- Beauty World - Hair

This is not just about choosing a topic. It's about claiming a space. You don't need to force this, just listen inward and look around. Your world is often already speaking to you.

Questions to ask:

- Who do I naturally attract?
- Who am I passionate about helping?
- Where do I have credibility or a transformational story?

- Where do I have both life experience and spiritual authority?
- What world does my spirit say I must serve?

Your Notes:

Section 2: Look at Your Story

Your life leaves clues.

Your personal and professional journey has carried you through specific seasons, industries, and communities for a reason. These experiences are golden and they hold the keys to building a speakerpreneur brand rooted in purpose, authenticity and power.

Start by simply recording your life story on your phone or voice recorder and descript that note into words using an app like descript.com. Talk like you're sharing it with a room full of people. Then, listen and read it back. As you do, ask the Lord to highlight the joy, the turning points, and the patterns. Ask for clarity on where you're called to serve in this current season.

This isn't just reflection… it's revelation.

Journal Prompts:

- What challenge have I overcome that others still struggle with? This determines if you have mastered this yet and at what level.

- What community or profession do I deeply understand?

- If I had to give one talk for the rest of my life, what would it be about and to whom, having what problem?

- If I had to choose one problem to solve for the next 10 years what would that be?

- What work do I want to be responsible "to deliver" for the rest of my life?

Your Notes:

_____

_____

_____

_____

_____

_____

_____

Section 3: Study the Industry Landscape

Once you have a few ideas about the potential "worlds" you're called to serve, it's time to research what already exists. Full-time speakers don't walk into industries blindly, we study them so we can enter with clarity and disrupt with excellence.

Here's what to do:

- Search top podcasts, books, and influencers in that space. Pay attention to the themes, messages, and conversations happening right now and generationally.

- Analyze what's missing. What's frustrating to you about the current voices or narratives? What feels overdone or underdeveloped?

- Define how your approach is different. What is your unique angle, your distinct perspective, your lived truth that separates you from the rest?

- Discern your commitment. Can you truly see yourself serving this space for a short season, a long time, or even a lifetime? Long time or lifetime preferred.

Remember: You don't need to be the first right now. You need to be the most aligned.

Keep these notes and all other questions and journal prompts to utilize in your content, speeches and other marketing materials.

Your Notes:

_____
_____
_____
_____
_____
_____
_____
_____

Section 4: You'll Commit to One World as the Focus (for Now)

Focus doesn't mean forever... but for now, you must treat your chosen world with full intention.

Each world deserves your clarity, energy, and excellence, because clarity attracts cash. Choosing one world to speak into gives you the chance to:

- Build authority faster
- Develop products and talks that resonate deeply
- Create raving fans who refer and repeat

Write down your decisions from a joyful place. At this moment you are not focusing on money. You are focusing on joy and alignment.

Review this statement below and create up to 5.

1. I choose to serve [audience] in the (or you could replace "in the" with "who have") [industry/world] through speaking, coaching, and transformational products.

_____

_____

_____

2. I choose to serve [audience] in the (or you could replace "in the" with "who have") [industry/world] through speaking, coaching, and transformational products.

_____

_____

_____

3. I choose to serve [audience] in the (or you could replace "in the" with "who have") [industry/world] through speaking, coaching, and transformational products.

_____

_____

4. I choose to serve **[audience]** in the (or you could replace "in the" with "who have") **[industry/world]** through speaking, coaching, and transformational products.

_____

_____

_____

5. I choose to serve **[audience]** in the (or you could replace "in the" with "who have") **[industry/world]** through speaking, coaching, and transformational products.

_____

_____

_____

Now Begin the Process of Elimination…

Take a moment to honestly review each world you've considered. Ask yourself:

Do I really want to do this?

Could I see myself serving in this space long-term (10 years min.) or even for life?

Did I overlook a world I'd love to be in? Let me pause and rethink.

Did I focus only on a narrow industry, or did I open myself up to a world of people?

Which of these brings me the most joy? Which feels the most aligned?

Once you've reflected…

Now choose **ONLY ONE**.

This is your focus.

This is your world.

And from here… we build.

Note your chosen world next:

(Write it clearly and confidently)

_____

_____

_____

_____

_____

Congratulations… you've claimed your lane.

If you feel confused and misaligned, take more time to reflect, or consider getting deeper support.

Go to **www.thespeakerpreneur.com** to be invited to our next speakerpreneur training and explore how we can help you further.

Release additional thoughts here.

_____

_____

_____

_____

_____

_____

_____

_____

_____

_____

_____

_____

_____

Section 5: Spiritual Alignment is Everything

You will make money fastest and in the healthiest way when you're operating where you feel most alive, most authentic, and most invested.

If you dread talking about your topic or don't genuinely care about your audience, no amount of marketing will save you from burnout or disappointment.

Tune in and ask yourself:

- Does this world and my decision excite me?
- Do I feel purpose and possibility in this space?
- Am I willing to stay consistent here for at least 10 years?
- Do I feel peace and passion when I think about serving here?
- Is this a space where I can show up authentically?
- Am I willing to stay faithful in this assignment even when results are slow?

Notice I keep asking similar questions to help you explore your previous decision deeply.

If your answers keep aligning, there's a good chance you're on the right path.

If not, that's okay… keep digging. Clarity is worth the work.

Remember this:

When your energy and industry match, momentum is inevitable.

Your Notes:

_____

_____

_____

_____

_____

Conclusion: Own Your Stage

Choosing your "world" isn't about limitation... it's about liberation.

It frees you to build a brand that connects, converts, and compounds.

When you boldly own your identity and your audience, the speaking opportunities, partnerships, and income will follow.

You're now positioned to stand out and speak up in a space that's uniquely yours.

I want to prepare your mind quickly as we get into several next steps that this process is structured to bring you into a space of positioning for all levels of pricing structures and offers.

A clear message and offer in the right world help you to get paid more because your speaking and expert message is targeted and focused.

The booker/potential client understands that you are worthy of high-ticket payment because your knowledge and skills align with high ticket value.

Every world and problem come with different tickets inside of it. In short, every problem has a price tag.

This is why many speakers stay low ticket, or struggle because they are positioned for general "motivational speaking" without an expert niche to match it.

They are essentially an "entertainment speaker".

When you don't have a solid space of expert value - a niche that positions you worthy of a "doctor" or "guru" seat, the booker struggles to prove a high-ticket value unless fame is highly attached to your brand.

Even then, if fame is attached and you have a high-ticket value knowledge base, your worth is absolutely undeniable.

Now, let's reflect and then go claim your title in the next step.

REFLECTION & ACTION TIME

Use this time to reflect over your notes, pray/meditate and make a plan of action from this step accordingly. Use an additional notebook if necessary, add dates and times to carry out the mission.

Goal | (Event that has Occurred in the spirit realm).

What is the specific goal or milestone you're focusing on right now?

_____

_____

_____

Steps Leading to the Goal

Break down the steps you need to take to reach this goal, one by one.

_____

_____

_____

Potential Obstacles

What might get in the way of you completing these steps?

_____

_____

_____

Support System

Who or what can help you overcome these obstacles or keep them manageable?

_____

_____

_____

STEP 3: YOUR SPEAKER IDENTITY – CLAIMING A TITLE THE WORLD UNDERSTANDS

Introduction: You Can't Be Paid for What You Won't Proclaim

Now that you're centered in purpose, let's bring clarity to how you introduce yourself to the world. Approach each section with the decision you made in the previous step. Use one of the following declarations to begin claiming your speakerpreneur identity with clarity and confidence:

- "I choose to serve **[audience]** in the **[industry/world]** through speaking, coaching, and transformational products."

Or

- "I choose to serve **[audience]** who have **[industry/world]** through speaking, coaching, and transformational products."

This is your foundation. Say it aloud. Own it. Refine it as needed… but commit to stating it boldly. In the business world, clarity creates currency. If people don't know or understand what you do or who you help, they can't hire you, refer you, or invest in your services. As a successful, growing speakerpreneur, you must boldly claim your identity and title with confidence, clarity, and strategy.

In my years of experience as a business advisor, I've seen too many people lead with hyper-unique titles like "Business Enthusiast of the Arts" and struggle to make consistent sales faster because their brand wasn't strong enough to support a title the world couldn't yet identify. Notice I said faster. You can make some sales, but consistency comes from building seniority and clear recognition.

The fastest way to accelerate your income is to go straight to the center of your ideal client's understanding. What are they searching for on Google? What title do they recognize that signals you can solve their problem? Find your "boring" unique title first, then add your personal flair after. I repeat: Yes, add the sprinkles, but lay the foundation with something obvious and relatable.

This step will guide you through identifying your speakerpreneur identity… a title that aligns with your vision and clearly communicates your value to your audience. Remember, you are a speaker in whatever field you choose. "Speaker" is an added title on top of the core business elements tied to your work. When your title reflects your purpose and positions you as a leader in your space, opportunities flow naturally and effortlessly.

I always say "speaking is to business, what lighter fluid is to a fire". Allow your speaking to set the rest of your products and services on fire!

Section 1: What is a Speakerpreneur Identity?

Your speakerpreneur identity is how you present yourself to the world as a professional, solution-driven expert. It's the clear, specific title and brand that tells people exactly what you do and how you help them.

Think about every high-income earner in the speaking world that you admire including myself. Whether they're a speaker, coach, consultant, or thought leader... their titles are specific. Not vague. Not wishy-washy. The value and transformation they provide is clear. Their title communicates:

- Who they help
- What they solve
- Why people should trust them

You need a title that helps your ideal audience instantly recognize you as the solution they've been searching for. This is about positioning, not perfection.

Let's start simple...

Right now, keep it straightforward and specific. Don't worry about being fancy just yet.

Try writing down a few clear titles that fit your focus.

Here are some Examples:

- Therapist to Traumatic Brain Injury Patients
- Math Tutor to children K-5
- Surgeon specializing in Neuroplasty

Remember your "I choose" & allow it to assist this process...

- I choose to serve **[audience]** in the (or you could replace in the with who have) **[industry/world]** through speaking, coaching, and transformational products.

Or

- I choose to serve **[audience]** who have **[industry/world]** through speaking, coaching, and transformational products.

Again, what would your ideal client type into Google to find someone like you?

Let that guide you.

This exercise is not about sounding impressive, it's about being discoverable and clear.

It's not just what you like – it's what your future client understands they need.

Here's a great starting point:

Prompt for AI or personal clarity:

"What type of mentor or expert is someone searching for if they struggle with **[insert industry or world issue]**?"

"What type of speaker is an event planner searching for if they are hiring for a crowd of [type of audience] who are **[insert industry or world issue]**?"

Write down a few prompts like that for yourself and jot the answers next to them.

Now, reflect and answer the questions below to build clarity:

- What tangible result do I help people achieve, that they would swim across the ocean for?

- What are the symptoms they experience?

- What are the main symptoms you will decide to serve?

- Based on the questions above, who is my audience?

- What type of expertise do I offer them?

- **As you go into the future - the 10 year from now you - and look back**... Ask yourself : What transformation or outcome am I best known for in my field of expertise?

Your Notes:

_____

_____

_____

_____

Section 2: Aligning Your Identity With Your Expertise

Now we can get a little fancy.

This section will help you reconfirm your earlier answers and begin layering in your uniqueness.

Your identity isn't about squeezing yourself into a mold... it's about carving out your lane and claiming it with confidence.

You're not just a speaker...

You're a personal brand.

You're walking purpose and impact.

You're an answered prayer.

You're a life-saving solution.

... and so much more.

But in order for others to experience that...

They need to know, clearly and simply, what you do... not just who you are.

In Step 2, you identified the space or "world" you're meant to serve. Now, it's time to create or re-think a simple "title message" that connects your experience, audience, and offer into a brand identity that's magnetic and monetizable. You may have already chosen this. Repeat if necessary.

Practice:

Play around with these few examples and see what funky nickname you might come up with for each. Sometimes, these kinds of creative titles work well for PR, branding, and storytelling. Think: The "X" Lady... The "X" Strategist.

- General Message: Helping professionals leave their 9-5s... Title: "Corporate Exit Strategist"
  Funky nickname title - the A.K.A. :

- General Message: Empowering creative entrepreneurs to scale through goods and services... Title: "Business Growth Consultant for Creatives"
  Funky nickname title - the A.K.A. :

- General Message: Teaching women in IT mindset hacks that make learning tech simple... Title: "High-Performance Mindset Coach for women in IT"
  Funky nickname title - the A.K.A. :

Note: You don't have to choose a funky title. Use this section only if it comes to you naturally or it's a major desire.

Try out a few variations below. Speak them aloud. Your winning title will feel both powerful and authentic.

Your Notes:

_____

_____

_____

_____

_____

_____

_____

_____

_____

_____

_____

_____

_____

_____

_____

_____

_____

_____

Section 3: Recapping & Adding On: Let's Create a Quick Bio +.

Language is leverage. The words you use to communicate with the world shapes how others perceive you... and just as importantly, how you perceive yourself.

Vague titles create confusion.

Specific, bold titles with clear extensions?

They command attention and open doors.

Never feel strange about owning a title. A title is simply a name...

And names carry power.

Jesus gave titles to His disciples.

God gave us names and the authority to name...

So don't take this part lightly.

Many pieces of your purpose, positioning, and prosperity are wrapped up in the names and titles you choose... or the ones you've avoided.

Choose the right ones.

Denounce the ones that no longer serve you.

We'll now start crafting your personal bio using the language you've uncovered in the steps above.

Let's go.

If you already have a speaker bio, check it now for structure and alignment.

If you don't have one yet, this is your moment to craft it with intention.

You'll want to create two versions:

A short bio (for quick intros, media kits, event pages)

A longer bio (for speaker one-sheets, websites, proposals)

The graph and breakout will help guide you.

But first, remember this:

People are drawn to precision and confidence.

Your words must match your ambition.

And don't worry about perfection right now.

Start where you are.

Get it on the page so we can keep momentum.

You'll always refine as you go. Let's move ahead.

What to Include in a Short Speaker Bio

Here is a basic layout of character count for different bios/marketing materials that will include parts of you speaker identity.

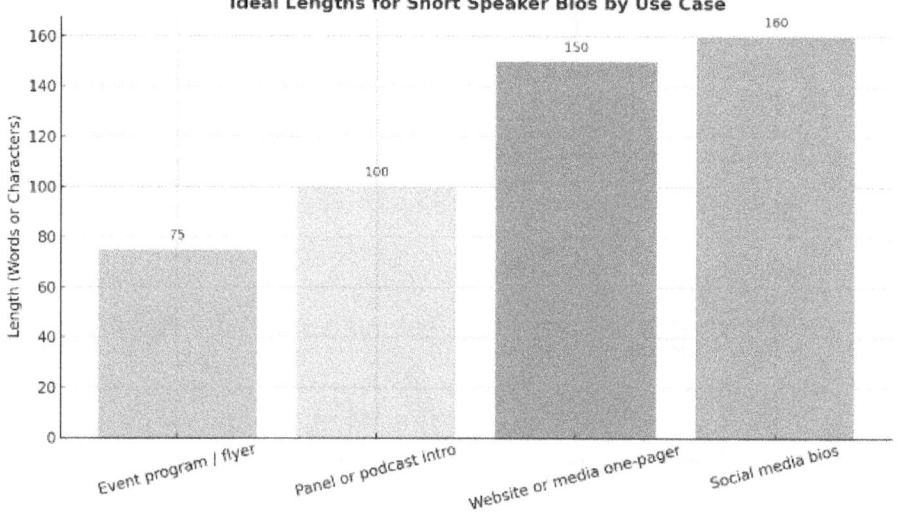

As for the speaker bio that is typically read by the moderator at events you speak on...

Here are a few key elements I recommend including:

1. **Full Name & Title** – e.g., *Jane Kelley, Speaker & Sales Strategist*

2. **What You Do** – Highlight your expertise (e.g., *helps faith-driven entrepreneurs master high-ticket sales through storytelling*).

3. **Key Achievements / Results** – Include a quantifiable win if space allows (e.g., *has helped over 1,000 speakers scale to 6 and 7 figures*).

4. **Personality / Brand Flavor** – A line that adds your vibe, especially if you're faith-based, fun, or fashion-forward.

5. **Optional CTA / Mention** – If applicable, include a mention of your website, podcast, or current project.

Your Turn - Notes:

_____
_____
_____
_____
_____
_____
_____
_____
_____
_____
_____
_____
_____
_____
_____
_____

Section 4: Owning Your Expertise Publicly

It's wild, but especially among what most would call "high-achieving men & women," there's often a tendency to downplay their skills outside of work... usually out of fear of being too bold.

But if you're going to master your realm of influence and step into a new level of financial abundance...

Visibility is non-negotiable.

Confidence attracts clients.

Clarity helps you close deals.

Don't wait for permission to accelerate. Be on the lookout for moments where you're stalling.

You don't need another certification, another title, or even another follower to tap into the game of business and impact.

And let's be real... you definitely don't need a certain follower count to position yourself as an expert.

Many of you already have everything you need, or you can grow over time.

What you do need is:

Evidence...

Experience...

And the belief that your voice is valuable.

Let me be clear: I'm not saying stop growing or learning.

But I am saying... maximize what you already have.

That's the key to owning your lane now, not later.

Affirmations if you need a boost in this are mentally:

- "I am the authority in my space."

- "My knowledge, story, and solutions are worthy of attention and investment."

- "I own my power and express it with clarity."

- "I was built and born for this position. It's my realm of genius."

Your Notes
_____
_____
_____
_____
_____
_____
_____
_____
_____
_____
_____
_____
_____
_____
_____
_____
_____
_____
_____
_____

Section 5: Bringing Your Identity to Life Across All Platforms

Once you've chosen your speaker identity, bring it to life across every customer touchpoint.

Consistency builds trust.

When people hear and see the same message repeatedly, they remember you, refer you, and invest because they have total clarity without distraction.

Apply your title and positioning clearly in places like:

- Social media bios
- LinkedIn headlines
- Business cards
- Website taglines
- Speaker Sheets
- Speaker Reels

(Visit www.speakerpreneur.com to receive other suggestions on what to include in your speaker reel, as well as your speaker sheet.)

Now It's Reflection time.

REFLECTION & ACTION TIME

Use this time to reflect over your notes, pray/meditate and make a plan of action from this step accordingly. Use an additional notebook if necessary, add dates and times to carry out the mission.

Goal | (Event that has Occurred in the spirit realm).

What is the specific goal or milestone you're focusing on right now?

_____

_____

_____

Steps Leading to the Goal

Break down the steps you need to take to reach this goal, one by one.

_____

_____

_____

Potential Obstacles

What might get in the way of you completing these steps?

_____

_____

_____

Support System

Who or what can help you overcome these obstacles or keep them manageable?

_____

_____

_____

STEP 4: AVATAR WORK – KNOWING WHO YOU'RE CALLED TO SERVE DEEPLY

Introduction: Your Audience Is the Key to Your Income

No matter how powerful your message, how polished your delivery, or how transformational your offer is, if it's not aligned with the right audience, it won't convert.

Financially independent speakerpreneurs don't aim for the masses.

They speak with such clarity and conviction to one person that it echoes across the thousands that one person represents.

This step is about identifying your ideal client — your avatar — with laser focus and deep understanding.

You've already started laying this foundation in earlier sections.

But here, we go deeper.

Because knowing exactly who you serve determines everything:

Your voice, your brand, your content, your pricing, your positioning and ultimately... your revenue, full-time status & staying power.

When you understand your avatar/audience better than they understand themselves, you don't just inspire them...

You lead them.

And when you're the obvious solution, abundance flows naturally.

So, let's get specific.

Section 1: The Power of Specificity

One of the biggest mistakes beginner speakers make is being too broad.

"I help people transform their lives."

"I speak to women who want more."

That kind of vagueness will keep your business stagnant and your bank account dry.

Specificity makes you searchable, referable, and magnetic.

Here's something I want you to hold on to. I've created two key terms to help you truly grasp this concept:

- Dynamic Specificity
- Broad Specificity

But before I break those down, let's touch on the popular phrase "niching down."

In speaking terms, niching down means focusing your message, brand, and marketing on a very specific group of people with a clear problem, identity, or desire — instead of trying to speak to everyone.

But I personally lean into something I call:

Niching In

"Niching in" aka Niching "Inward" - is a term I created dictating the process of aligning your message, mission, and audience by getting to the core of your God-ordained purpose, the present season of your assignment, and the unique skill set you've been given.

It's not just about picking a market...

It's about tuning into who you're truly meant to serve right now with precision, clarity, and spiritual obedience.

The work we've been doing in the previous steps up to this point is setting you up for that.

Now let's dig in to what I mean by dynamic specificity and broad specificity with practical examples in the next section.

Dynamic Specificity – Definition

Dynamic Specificity is the strategic, intentional act of focusing your message, marketing, and offers on a highly defined individual or group... with clear lifestyle details, mindset patterns, and specific struggles.

You're not just solving a surface problem... it feels like you're reading their journal.

This level of specificity positions you as a specialist rather than a generalist, building deeper trust, increasing your perceived value, and allowing you to charge premium prices.

You speak directly to one, and it resonates with many.

Example:

(*Deep, emotionally resonant, hyper-targeted phrasing.*)

"I help high-performing women of color in tech who second-guess every take, overthink their delivery, and hesitate to hit 'post'... finally create magnetic, camera-ready content that feels powerful, authentic, and professional."

Broadened Specificity – Definition

Broadened Specificity means zoning in on a clear, specific type of person, but solving a problem that is shared across a much larger, more mainstream population. Your audience still feels seen, but the solution you offer has mass appeal.

This approach positions you as a scalable messenger, giving you the ability to reach and convert wider audiences while still sounding personal.

Example:

(*Wider appeal while still identifying a clear audience.*)

"I help high-achieving women of color who feel pressure to 'show up perfectly' online create confident, polished content and training videos that reflect their expertise."

Use dynamic specificity to dominate a niche and speak directly to a high-converting segment.

Use broadened specificity when your solution is relevant to many, but you still want to sound like you "get" a particular audience.

Many times, dynamic specificity can be very useful when converting advanced, high-ticket audiences.

Broadened specificity, many times appeal to massive amounts of beginner and low-ticket audiences.

Also, here are examples of a few random, specific avatars:

- Mid-career 40+ women in tech who want to transition into coaching
- Stay-at-home moms launching an online business
- Men over 40 struggling with fitness after burnout
- Creative entrepreneurs scaling past six figures

The more specific you get either way, the faster you grow. Just note: Both are specific. Jot down any notes you have below.

_____

_____

_____

_____

_____

_____

_____

_____

_____

_____

_____

_____

_____

_____

_____

_____

_____

Section 2: Avatar Traits – The Good and the Bad

To build a powerful, accurate profile of your ideal client, you must go beyond surface-level demographics. Age, job title, and location are just a starting point... not the full picture.

True connection comes when you understand:

Their deepest aspirations

Their day-to-day frustrations

And most importantly... the real-life consequences of those frustrations.

Ask yourself:

What is happening in their life because of the problem they haven't solved yet?

That's where your message becomes magnetic.

When you can articulate their inner world better than they can, they'll trust you to lead them out of it. That's where transformation and business begins.

You want both their good and bad traits. Good for you – Bad for the problem you'll take care of. Here are a few examples.

Possible Good traits (for you):

- Driven and success-minded
- Invests in personal growth
- Looks for transformation, not just information
- Spiritually curious or success conscious
- Respects experts and mentors

Possible Bad traits (what frustrates them):

- Overwhelmed with free content
- Distrusts programs due to past experiences
- Thinks they know it all, but lacks results

- Has shiny object syndrome

Possible Life happenings (issues that arise due to bad traits):

- Arguing with children and husband (due to bad trait and how)

- Boss increasing workload which takes away mental health time (due to bad trait and how)

- Insomnia unable to sleep which is making them late to work (due to bad trait and how)

Questions to ask yourself:

- What keeps them up at night, tossing and turning?

- What do they secretly wish someone would help them solve?

- What do they hate about their current options?

When you know not just their pain points, but their deepest desires and the life symptoms that come from them… your content, offers, and speeches will hit differently.

(They won't just hear you…

They'll feel you.)

Section 3: What Is Your Avatar Googling?

We're here again lol... Because this is a game-changer!

Your ideal client is already searching for answers... you need to position yourself as the result host to their question.

Exercise:
Imagine your avatar is typing into Google:

- "How to build confidence after a career break"

- "Christian speaker for women entrepreneurs"

- "What to charge as a new consultant"

- "Why am I stuck in my business?"

Knowing and using this also puts you in a good position to utilize SEO (Search Engine Optimization) which we may touch on later.

The Google searches happening in your world or industry are a goldmine of prompts for creating content, titling speeches, and naming your offers.

Use these to:

- Create highly clickable YouTube, podcast and/or social media titles

- Design compelling disruptive opt-in freebies, lead magnets that pull them in heavily

- Build speech frameworks that speak to real-time needs and also tell stories that mirror them

- (Another avatar you have is also the booking agent looking for a speaker in your world) Set a google alert for one who may place an advertisement for a speaker in your niche.

Section 4: Your Avatar's Emotional Landscape

People buy emotionally and logically. To convert consistently, you need to understand your avatar's emotional journey, and then connect logic to it. Logic, both emotional and practical, also helps you overcome objections during the sales process.

What they feel — and what objections might arise from it:

Feeling : Frustrated by their current limitations
- What logical objections might they raise because of this frustration?

Feeling : Inspired by success stories but unsure if it's possible for them.
- What limiting beliefs or doubts could logically come up here?

Intimidated by investing but curious
- What financial fears or past experiences might hold them back?

Torn between their comfort zone and their calling
- What internal conflict or perceived risk could delay their decision?

Speak to these emotions & their logic across every touchpoint:

- Sales pages

- Instagram captions & video reels

- Webinar pitches

- Podcast interviews

Suggestions of language to utilize:

- "I know you're tired of…"

- "If you're the kind of woman who…"

- "You've tried everything, but still feel like…"

Use empathetic marketing, not manipulative marketing. Root your message in truth and emotional clarity… not guilt. Highlight the consequences of staying stuck while painting a powerful picture of what's possible.

Note: These emotional & logical tensions are often where the strongest objections live. Especially in high-ticket, transformation-based industries. Address them with authenticity, compassion and clarity.

Types of product/general service Objections and Their Strategic Insights

1. Money Objections

Examples:

- "I can't afford it right now."
- "That's too expensive for me."
- "Do you offer a discount or payment plan?"

The Root Cause Here:
Fear of not seeing a return on investment. Often stems from a scarcity mindset or past financial trauma.

Your Reframe Should:
Help the prospect shift from cost-thinking to value-thinking. Emphasize what the transformation is worth, not just the price tag.

Write your response here (grade after if it truly shifts the objection):

_____

_____

_____

_____

_____

_____

2. Time Objections

Examples:

- "I'm too busy right now."
- "I want to do it later."
- "This isn't the right season for me."

The Root Cause Here:
Overwhelm, poor prioritization, or avoidance of commitment. Often reflects internal misalignment, not actual lack of time.

Write your response here (grade after if it truly shifts the objection):

_____

_____

_____

_____

_____

_____

3. Self-Doubt Objections

Examples:

- "What if I fail?"
- "I'm not sure I can follow through."
- "I've tried other things that didn't work."

The Root Cause Here:
Fear of failure, imposter syndrome, or lack of confidence in their ability to succeed... even if they trust you.

Write your response here (grade after if it truly shifts the objection):

_____

_____

_____

_____

4. Family Dynamic Objections

Examples:

- "I need to ask my spouse."

- "My family wouldn't support this."

- "My kids/job/lifestyle won't allow it."

The Root Cause Here:
Desire for permission or validation. Fear of disrupting home life or making decisions that challenge family expectations.

Write your response here (grade after if it truly shifts the objection):

_____

_____

_____

_____

_____

_____

5. Trust Objections

Examples:

- "I need to think about it."

- "How do I know this will work for me?"

- "I've been burned before."

- "Have you ever worked with someone like me?"

Root Cause:
Uncertainty about your credibility, the offer's effectiveness, or their belief in the process.

Write your response here (grade after if it truly shifts the objection):

_____

_____

_____

_____

Types of Speaker Service Objections and Their Strategic Insights

If you are pitching to engagements, those that are hiring you will mostly share your same audience objections, you must remember to handle their objections for you as a speaker as well, though.

1. "Your fee is higher than we expected."

What they're really saying:
They're unclear on the value you bring, or they haven't budgeted for your level of expertise.

Reframe:
Price is never the real issue... value is. Elevate the conversation from cost to ROI.

Write your response here (grade after if it truly shifts the objection):

_____

_____

_____

_____

2. "We're already booked this year" or "It's too late/early in our planning cycle."

What they're really saying:
They don't feel urgency, or they're unsure how to fit you into their calendar.

Reframe:
High-impact speakers *create* opportunities... they don't wait for perfect timing.

Write your response here (grade after if it truly shifts the objection):

_____

_____

_____

3. "We've already hired a speaker."

What they're really saying:
They don't see how you fit in *addition* to their current choice, or your message feels redundant.

Reframe:
Different angles create a deeper impact. Think collaboration, not competition.

Write your response here (grade after if it truly shifts the objection):

_____
_____
_____
_____

4. **"Our audience might not resonate with your style or background."**

What they're really saying:
They're unsure if you're the right cultural or demographic fit... or they're risk-averse.

Reframe:
You don't need to be everything to everyone... you need to be unforgettable to the right audience.

Write your response here (grade after if it truly shifts the objection):

_____
_____
_____
_____

5. **"Can you send me a proposal or video, and we'll circle back?"**

What they're really saying:
They're brushing you off, or they need more proof before seriously considering you.

Reframe:
The follow-up *is* the fortune. Don't leave it open-ended, anchor a next step.

Write your response here (grade after if it truly shifts the objection):

_____
_____

6. "What if this doesn't land with our people?"

What they're really saying:
They're scared of wasting time, money, or credibility on a speaker that flops.

Reframe:
Eliminate doubt by highlighting results and outcomes, not just delivery style.

Write your response here (grade after if it truly shifts the objection):

7. "We're not sure this fits the theme."

What they're really saying:
They don't yet see how your message supports their agenda.

Reframe:
Themes can flex when aligned with transformation. Show how your talk *enhances* the theme.

Write your response here (grade after if it truly shifts the objection):

Section 5: Interview Your Avatar

The best data doesn't just come from analytics... it comes from *conversations*.

These can also be sales call gatherings, pitch responses, or any resources where people who have bought these types of products/services gather to give insight and experience. This can also be achieved from sites like Quora or Reddit.

You can also gather data from others' statements on these apps that are aligned with your business and what you provide

Interview 5-10 people who fit your ideal client profile. Ask them:

- What are your biggest goals this year?
- What's stopping you from reaching them?
- What have you tried that hasn't worked?
- What would make you say YES to a speaker/coach/product?

If you are interviewing speaking (organizers/bookers): :

- What are the top three qualities you look for in a speaker you hire?
- When you think of the *best speaker* you've ever hired, what made them memorable?
- What kind of experience do you want your audience to walk away with? (e.g., motivation, transformation, practical steps, energy)
- What specific goals or outcomes do you expect a speaker to help you achieve?
- How do you define a "successful" speaking engagement?
- Which speaking styles do you prefer? (e.g., storytelling, data-driven, motivational, interactive)
- Do you prefer speakers who customize their message to your audience or deliver signature talks?
- How important is it that the speaker blends education with entertainment?

- What topics or themes are most in demand for your events right now?

- What *don'ts* or turn-offs do you have when it comes to speaker delivery or message?

- What factors most influence your decision to hire a speaker? (e.g., price, reputation, social proof, niche expertise)

- What is your typical budget range for speakers?

- How far in advance do you typically book speakers?

- Do you prefer virtual, in-person, or hybrid speakers?

- How do you usually find the speakers you book? (e.g., referrals, speaker bureaus, social media, direct outreach)

- What makes you feel excited or confident about hiring a new speaker?

- What worries or hesitations do you have when booking a speaker?

- If a speaker could solve one big problem for your event or audience, what would it be?

- What would make a speaker irresistible to you or your planning team?

- If you could wave a magic wand and create your dream speaker experience, what would it look and feel like?

Record the answers on the next page. These are your marketing materials.

Conclusion: Build for Her/He/Corporation, Not for Likes

You're not here just to go viral. You're here to serve, transform, and build wealth while doing it. When you know your avatar deeply, you stop guessing and start creating content, offers, and speeches that convert consistently.

Get obsessed with understanding your avatar's world. Build products & services they actually want... ones they would drop everything for. Speak directly to your avatar's heart. When you do that, your business becomes unstoppable.

In the next section, we'll focus on creating your irresistible offer... the solution your avatar has been waiting for.

Now It's Reflection time. Feel free to add any additional thoughts here.

_____

_____

_____

_____

_____

_____

_____

_____

_____

_____

_____

_____

_____

_____

_____

REFLECTION & ACTION TIME

Use this time to reflect over your notes, pray/meditate and make a plan of action from this step accordingly. Use an additional notebook if necessary, add dates and times to carry out the mission.

Goal | (Event that has Occurred in the spirit realm).

What is the specific goal or milestone you're focusing on right now?

_____

_____

_____

Steps Leading to the Goal

Break down the steps you need to take to reach this goal, one by one.

_____

_____

_____

Potential Obstacles

What might get in the way of you completing these steps?

_____

_____

_____

Support System

Who or what can help you overcome these obstacles or keep them manageable?

_____

_____

_____

STEP 5: OFFER – DESIGNING A TANGIBLE, SALIVATING SOLUTION

Introduction: Your Offer Is the Engine of Your Business

Your offer is the tangible expression of the transformation you promise… and the tangible expression of the transformation you're anointed to deliver.

It's how you convert your expertise, story, and skills into a product or service that solves real problems and generates real revenue.

A powerful offer doesn't just describe what you do… it positions you as the go-to expert in your space.

The two sides of the offer are:

What can you do for me? (the result you deliver), and

Who are you? (your identity).

High-performing, financially independent speakerpreneurs don't just hope people understand their value…

They strategically design offers that speak directly to their audience's deepest needs and most urgent goals.

This step walks you through how to do exactly that.

Note that as you go through this keep in mind the difference between an offer & a product/service:

Product or Service = The Product or Service says, "this is the way I'm delivering this promise to you".

The **actual thing** your client is paying for. The delivery format of what you sell.

- **Product**: A tangible or digital item (e.g., a book, course, workbook, online training)
- **Service**: A skill or support you provide (e.g., 1-on-1 coaching, keynote speaking, consulting). Think of the **product or service** as the **vehicle** that delivers the result.

Offer = The Offer says, "this is what I can guarantee you and promise you". It's How You Package & Present What You Sell…

An **offer** is the **bundle + messaging + pricing + value** around your product or service that makes someone say, "YES, I need that!"

Your **offer** includes:

- The product/service itself

- Bonuses or extras (e.g., templates, a free or low ticket call, group support)

- Pricing and payment options

- Delivery format (live, recorded, in-person, etc.)

- A clear promise/result

- A deadline or incentive (limited-time, fast-action bonus, etc.)

The offer is what makes the sale happen. It's not just *what* you sell... it's *how* you position and present it so it feels irresistible and results-driven.

So again...

The offer says, "this is what I can guarantee you and promise you" and the product or service says, "this is the way". That's the difference. Some people say the offer is the product and service, but it is not the product and service. The offer answers "what are you going to do for me". The product and service answer "how are you going to do the offer for me?"... (i.e. through this way, through this method.) The product and service is however a part of the offer.

Ok, let's go.

Your Notes:

_____

_____

_____

_____

_____

_____

_____

_____

_____

Section 1: Focus on the Transformation You Deliver

People don't buy coaching, courses, or speeches.

They buy results, safety, and security.

Your offer must clearly define the outcome the client will experience.

Your audience is silently asking:

What's in it for me?

Why should I trust you?

What will it cost me if I don't listen to you?

Examples:

- "You'll walk away with a fully developed launch plan for your brand to increase by 90% in revenue and viewers ."

- "You'll rebuild your confidence to land your next 6 figure promotion and create a clear roadmap for your pitch."

- "You'll learn how to secure high-paying speaking opportunities in your niche within 30 days."

Speaker Tip: Start by identifying the pain point and the symptoms that the pain is causing that your client wants solved. Then build your offer as the bridge from that problem to their desired result/desire.

Your Notes:

_____

_____

_____

_____

Section 2: Solve a Real Problem with Strategic Structure

Speakerpreneurs are solution designers.

They think like architects.

Your offer should host a system or process that helps your client achieve their goal faster, easier, and with less confusion and energy exerted.

One of the easiest ways to clarify your message and offers is to **think in terms of a formula**.

In my trainings, I often describe a formula as the **foundational, step-by-step process** you use to guide someone from where they're stuck to the transformation you help them achieve.

Think of it like helping someone **cross a bridge**—on one side, they're overwhelmed and unsure; by the time they reach the other side, they feel clear, confident, and equipped. Or imagine helping them **step across a rocky river**, landing on each stone with purpose until they reach solid ground.

Once you've created your formula, it becomes the **blueprint for everything else**. You can turn it into a course, a keynote, a coaching program, or even a book... and the best part? It's always authentic and original... because it's based on *your* process, not anyone else's.

Note : You will refer back to this formula many times.

To help in your formula creation ask yourself:

- What pain and symptoms are my audience experiencing?
- What steps did I personally take to solve it?
- What shortcuts, tools, or insights can I offer to make their journey easier?
- What is my client Googling to solve this? (Think with an SEO mindset.)

Structure your offer's overall formula like a clear roadmap. Every step that it takes to take your client from problem to solution should be clearly outlined.

Think frameworks, phases, and predictable results.

Strategy builds trust. Simplicity builds sales.

Section 3: Build an Offer Around Your Zone of Genius

Your most profitable offer will come from what you do best, not just what's trending. Don't force your gifts into a format that drains you. Instead, build offers that match how you work best.

Now I must admit... this goes very deep. Like extremely deep.

You're not just creating an offer that goes into a program or product.

You're creating your lifestyle and an experience for yourself and the client you will serve.

You're taking your spirit and soul, then combining it with the physical work/world through service.

Like what???

Yeah.

Thankfully, this guide is designed so that you've already started this work in the steps prior to this.

Truthfully, most of my money comes from helping people craft these offers because high-achieving unique humans with so many diverse skills and talents often struggle to choose what should be done now vs. later... or wait until they're burned out to pivot.

Everything can be done.

But timing is the key.

If you need more help with this, visit **www.thespeakerpreneur.com** fill out the form to work with myself & our team of experts.

We likely have a paid workshop, intensive, or 1-on-1 opportunity somewhere near you to help get this mess out the way so you can begin serving at your highest capacity. We'll get back to you ASAP.

As for the moment. Here are a few offer formats. These are products/services:

- A 6-week group coaching program
- A VIP day or half-day strategy session
- A 90-day 1-on-1 mentorship
- A self-paced course with built-in accountability
- A book
- A monthly subscription

Keep it simple.

Define what the client gets, how long it takes, what's included, and the result they can expect.

If you can explain your offer in one or two sentences — it's ready.

It MUST be attractive to the one of many who needs it though.

A few things to ask yourself & then place your notes below:

- What offer don't I mind enduring stress for?
- If I was obligated to do this as a job, would I love my job?
- Does this align with the items I wrote in the previous steps that coincide with my mission, purpose and what I love to do in some way? My world…

_____

_____

_____

_____

_____

_____

_____

Section 4: Price with Confidence and Logic

Your price for the products and services within your offer communicates your positioning. Underpricing or overpricing doesn't attract more clients... it undermines your credibility. I believe in pricing in levels and tiers.

My process is simple: no one should be able to say "no" to you without having something to walk away with. There should be a meaningful offer at every price point.

I also believe — especially as a speaker — your offer should have both B2C (Business-to-Consumer) and B2B (Business-to-Business) capability. Let's look at few pointers when pricing:

- Base your pricing on the *value* you're delivering, not necessarily on the hours involved.

- Consider the cost of inaction for your client... what does it cost them not to solve this problem?

- Position your price as an investment, not an expense. Speak to the return, not just the rate.

- Be realistic about your current situation. Making deals is a natural part of business. You're not completely stuck to a base price, but you do need to be committed to one when entering negotiations.

    Everyone is in a different space and financial situation, including you.

    When negotiating, consider:

- What is the lowest you will go and what is the highest you will go.

- What is the lowest you're willing to go?

Add additional notes here.

_____

_____

_____

_____

Also, ask yourself honestly:
- How sharp are my skills?

- If they ask me to deliver everything inside this product or service… can I execute it with excellence?

- Do I need to improve in any areas (e.g., Photoshop, leadership, sales)?

- Can I quickly find answers or resources to fill the gaps?

- Do I need to bring in a trusted outsourcer to support the quality of delivery?

- Do I need a trusted outsourcer?

Suggested Pricing Tiers:

First off… You may want to make an overall basis of what your offer itself is worth usually worth in the industry and how…

Note that as the years go by & depending on your niche and other factors this is quite likely to change here and there.

As you get to pricing products and services…

Use tiered pricing to build momentum & trust — low-ticket to introduce & transform, mid-ticket to deepen engagement + skill building & transform, and high-ticket to speed up time & deliver transformation.

I like to say everyone who is assigned to you should walk away with something bought. These are just a few ideas that I will bring back later in another step…

- Free / Low-Ticket ($0–$197+): eBooks, PDFs, workshops, digital templates — great for introduction, access, and early transformation.

- Mid-Ticket ($297–$997+): Group programs, live intensives, or self-paced courses — designed for deeper engagement, community learning, and skill development.

- High-Ticket ($1,500+): Private coaching, VIP strategy sessions, done-for-you services, or masterminds — this is where you offer speed, structure, and results.

- Premium / B2B High-Level ($10K+): Corporate packages, licensing, long-term consulting or facilitation — positioned for companies, school districts, or high-capacity leaders ready to scale with your expertise.

I want to mention a few tips here for speaking offers – specifically towards pricing acceptance and inquiry. I'll go a bit deeper into pitching later in this guide. You must make it very clear who you are when you are networking for engagement opportunities, or asked at any time what you do. When negotiating price, always ask unless it's specified…If specified then confirm.

Don't ask "Is this a paid opportunity?" … This could allude to a fact that you take non paying opportunities… and you are NOT. Instead you should ask… "What is the budget for speakers?" When you ask this… The coordinator/planner could say a few different things…

Usually, it's these responses… "The budget is…" "I Don't know…" or "I'm not a privilege to say…". Every once in a blue moon you may hear… "Well, what do you normally charge?"

If they say they don't have a budget and want to get your take, ask them… "What is the budget you paid your speakers last year?" This will help you to determine the rate that you should pitch to them. In other general notes you must always factor in the fees of accepting this engagement in your pricing. Parking, travel, food, hotel, time commitment, etc. I advise doing a profit/loss analysis. If you have done research on the event (which you should have) and found that the budget was $2,000,000 or more… Then usually you know they have room to pay you upwards of $5k - $20k+.

P.S. If you plan to be a global speaker… Get your passport now, if you don't have it already. Be ready for international travel and start thinking about who would travel with you etc. This matters for budget, pricing, protection and so much more. Never have expired documents and always have your travel gear pre-packed and ready to go at any time.

Section 5: Market the Offer as a Catalyst for Change

Your offer isn't just "nice to have." It's a powerful vehicle for change — TODAY.

When you position it properly, your audience will see it as a must-have solution for their right-now problem.

Don't just sell tomorrow's transformation.

Sell from a "now-change" standpoint.

What happens immediately when they say yes?

Shift your mindset:

- Selling is spiritual. My selling is a seed planted into the future of the soil for the consumer.

- You are not just selling — you're solving and doctoring.

- You're not just "pitching" — you're forging and presenting a clear path forward.

- You're not convincing anyone! — You're communicating value and confirming (or denying) suspicions they already had.

Use your message, testimonials, and brand presence to reinforce that your offer is:

- Built to create momentum

- Positioned to solve problems

- Designed to upgrade lifestyles

When **your** people experience you, they should immediately feel:

"I need this now."

Conclusion: Build, Package, and Sell with Purpose

Our offer is the heartbeat… alongside traffic of your business.

When it's clear, strategic, and aligned with both your strengths and your audience's needs, sales feel natural… because they are.

Revenue becomes predictable.

Growth becomes scalable.

This is how speakerpreneurs shift from inconsistent income to sustainable success and ultimately, financial freedom.

In the next step, we'll dive into crafting your core message… the magnetic narrative that anchors your brand and attracts your ideal clients.

Now it's reflection time.

REFLECTION & ACTION TIME

Use this time to reflect over your notes, pray/meditate and make a plan of action from this step accordingly. Use an additional notebook if necessary, add dates and times to carry out the mission.

Goal | (Event that has Occurred in the spirit realm).

What is the specific goal or milestone you're focusing on right now?

_____

_____

_____

Steps Leading to the Goal

Break down the steps you need to take to reach this goal, one by one.

_____

_____

_____

Potential Obstacles

What might get in the way of you completing these steps?

_____

_____

_____

Support System

Who or what can help you overcome these obstacles or keep them manageable?

_____

_____

_____

STEP 6: CLEAR MESSAGE – WHAT YOU STAND FOR AND HOW IT ALIGNS WITH YOUR OFFER

Introduction: Your Message Should be a Reflection of Your Divine Assignment + A Bold Initiative Within Your Marketing Power

Your message is the heartbeat of your brand.

It's the bold statement that communicates what you stand for, what you believe, and why your work matters.

In a crowded marketplace, it's not the loudest speaker who wins — it's the clearest, the most precise — the one who permeates truth and understanding throughout the minds, hearts, and souls of the people.

Clarity converts.

Financially independent speakerpreneurs understand that message drives momentum.

When your message is aligned, consistent, as well as emotionally & logically resonant… it attracts the right clients, opens the right doors, and sets you apart from the noise.

This step will help you articulate the core message attached to your brand so that every word you speak or write is strategic and powerful.

Section 1: Define What You Stand For

Start with your values, beliefs, and unique perspective. Your message should be bigger than a service, it should be rooted in a worldview.

Ask yourself:

- What belief do I have that contradicts what's commonly taught in my industry?

- What do I *refuse* to be silent about?

- What change do I want to see in my audience's lives/businesses etc. from what I am providing?
    - Then… how can this align with my brand?
    - Is the change I am proposing attractive to what my potential clients ALSO want to see?

- What are my philosophical stances on life and life topics that coincide with the person as whole in the world I've chosen to be a part of.

Simple Example: "I believe that women don't need to choose between luxury and purpose. Most people teach otherwise. When you move in purpose, it helps to align with missions that push you into luxury and joy at the same time. Let's build both, because one without the other can cause fatigue and dissatisfaction… conforming to a non-holistic lifestyle. Luxury is health!" (add proof to this with statistics)

Bold messages spark curiosity, respect, and connection. Don't water yours down to be liked. Amplify it to be unforgettable.

On the flip side you will need to also consider the other part of the message.

1. What can I actually tangibly do for them? (we worked on this in prior lessons)

2. Like… simply… What are they even hiring me for?

#2 is a huge part that people get stuck in. If you continue to revert to what you *"feel"* your person *"needs to understand" "needs to know"* or the process they *"should be focusing on"* you have skipped past the whole meaning of servant hood and in turn trashed your sales.

You have become a narcissistic seller – and a selfish seller… You don't want that.

The funnel from top to back should have these parts of the message in mind…

- What does my consumer need or think they need to pay for right now?
- Who does my consumer think or know they need to hire right now?
- What does my audience actually believe?

Now… you can develop a relationship based on this and earn the right to move into a deeper connection…

- What repels my audience from me and on the flip side what engages and pulls them in closer to me &/or my product/service?
- How can I offer my product and service to them now as the solution to this issue. What's my winning formula?

Note here…

Your most authentic self will repel a person or draw them in.

Don't ask only "who do I want to attract"?… ask "who do I want to be around on a consistent basis"? Does my message align with this? Place your notes below.

_____
_____
_____
_____
_____
_____
_____
_____
_____
_____
_____
_____

Section 2: Connect Your Message to Your Offer

Your message isn't just about inspiration... it should lead people directly into your solution.

Alignment is key. If your message is about empowerment, but your offer doesn't deliver confidence, clarity, or tools, your brand feels disconnected. When your offer is the practical outcome of your message, potential clients naturally say yes.

Bridge Example:

- Message: "Women with timid voices are not necessarily timid, they are constrained by trauma. I help them define that trauma and rediscover the boldness in their speaking voice to land high paying speaking engagements."

- Offer & Product: In 6 weeks you'll be positioned to execute as a powerful speaker and have spoken at 4 paid engagements. This is a 6-week speaking confidence bootcamp that will cause the room to never forget you or your message.

Your audience should be able to see the direct link between what you say and what you sell.

Your Notes:

_____
_____
_____
_____
_____
_____
_____
_____
_____
_____
_____
_____
_____

Section 3: Craft a Messaging Statement

Create a powerful, 1–2 sentence message that acts as your brand's north star. This should appear on your website, bio, pitch decks, and introductions.

Formula:
"I believe [what you stand for]. I help [ideal audience] achieve [result] through [your offer/approach]."

Example:
"I believe high-achieving women deserve to build wealth with their voice. I help corporate professionals transition into profitable speaker brands through strategic offers and high-converting content."

This message makes it easy for others to remember you, refer to you, see exactly what the end will be when working with you and trust your brand & it's not fancy, but overall it's clear.

Try yours here along with any other notes you'd like to jot down:

_____

_____

_____

_____

_____

_____

_____

_____

_____

_____

_____

_____

_____

_____

Section 4: Use Your Message Everywhere

Once you've created your message, don't hide it... *repeat it.*

Ways to use your message:

- Social media bios and captions
- Email signatures
- Website headers
- Speaker one-sheets and media kits
- Podcast intros
- Event pitches and interviews

Repetition builds recognition. And recognition builds trust. Here's a note space.

_____
_____
_____
_____
_____
_____
_____
_____
_____
_____
_____
_____
_____
_____

Section 5: Refine and Reiterate

Your message isn't set in stone... it evolves as your business grows. Stay consistent in your core belief but be open to refining how you say it as you better understand your audience and your positioning.

Audit your message every quarter:

- Is it still aligned with your current offer?
- Does it reflect where your brand is headed?
- Is it resonating with the right people?

As you move forward in business—especially in the early stages of growth and expansion—you may feel the urge to change your offer and message frequently. It's normal to tweak when launching a new offer, starting a business, or defining (or redefining) your message. However, if you find yourself drastically changing your audience more than 30 to 50 times while following this guide, it's a sign you've stepped away from your commitment to who you're meant to serve right now.

This process of working through the guide is designed to help you ask, re-ask, and revisit questions in different ways so you can land firmly on your true purpose and chosen service world. Sometimes, you'll discover that the world chooses you before you choose it.

Don't be afraid to make edits... just be prayerful and intentional. And never stay vague. Once you find something that works, lean into building it rather than completely changing course... unless your spirit clearly directs you otherwise.

Refer back to previous steps in this guide to ensure your tweaks keep you on the right path every time you reevaluate.

Your Notes:

_____
_____
_____
_____
_____
_____
_____

Conclusion: Your Message is the Magnet

A clear message isn't a luxury… it's a necessity.

It draws in the right people, filters out the wrong ones, and positions you as a thought leader worth listening to.

It's the core of your mission.

When your message and your offer work in harmony, your business grows with ease and alignment.

In the next step, we'll talk about building a magnetic personal brand that visually and emotionally reflects your message and expertise.

Now It's Reflection time.

REFLECTION & ACTION TIME

Use this time to reflect over your notes, pray/meditate and make a plan of action from this step accordingly. Use an additional notebook if necessary, add dates and times to carry out the mission.

Goal | (Event that has Occurred in the spirit realm).

What is the specific goal or milestone you're focusing on right now?

_____

_____

_____

Steps Leading to the Goal

Break down the steps you need to take to reach this goal, one by one.

_____

_____

_____

Potential Obstacles

What might get in the way of you completing these steps?

_____

_____

_____

Support System

Who or what can help you overcome these obstacles or keep them manageable?

_____

_____

_____

STEP 7: BRAND IDENTITY – BECOMING THE GO-TO VOICE & VISION IN YOUR SPACE

Introduction: Your Brand Is What They Remember and Repeat

Your brand identity creates the emotional and visual connection people have with your business.

It tells your audience who you are, what you stand for, and why they should trust you... all before you ever say a word.

Like it or not, your brand is what people see you as... not necessarily how you see yourself.

It's the stereotype or association your audience has formed based on their interaction with your presence, content, and messaging.

Full-time speakerpreneurs understand that a powerful brand builds trust, authority, impact... and therefore, income.

This step will help you build a personal brand that is authentic, strategic, and memorable.

When done intentionally, your brand becomes your reputation, your leverage, and your magnet.

How does your audience see your current brand? What type of feelings or engagement is associated with your brand from the lens of your audience?

Your Notes:

_____

_____

_____

_____

_____

_____

_____

_____

_____

Section 1: What Do You Want to Be Known For?

Start with the end in mind. Every elite brand is rooted in clarity. Ask yourself & write out:

- What do I want people to associate with my name - then my look - then my personality?

- What is the emotional experience I want to create?

- What transformation am I the go-to for? (If one wants a specific thing done, go to this person)

- When I look ahead 10 years from now what transformation is my name now associated with from the work I've done in this business?

- What did the audience say the work did for them both tangible and emotionally?

Your brand is your positioning. It should be based on strategy, not just mere trends. Own the lane you want to dominate. If you are not willing to own it for several years (I recommend at least 10) and push it - you may want to reevaluate if you even want to do it.

You will come to notice that I believe in being extremely intentional about time frames and time mapping.

You won't always be perfect in your timeframe and time mapping. Having something to work with though… such as a thought process around life's happenings, will always help you to have a basis of safety & security. It opens doors to maneuver the desires of your heart towards God's full plan for your life.

Many times, the real problem in our lives lies in the fact that we depend on God for our every desire and need… when He has already placed desires within us, according to Scripture.

We are more in control of what happens to us… and what doesn't—than we often give God credit for. Remember He created and empowered man as His supernatural children.

You also may want to look at the work you did in the other steps.

You may have strayed again from the core values you set at the beginning of these parts. Every vision takes a war to begin and a revolution + revelations to keep it going. So if this did happen, know that you can get right back on track by revisiting the steps.

Section 2: Design with Intention

Visuals matter.

People buy with their eyes and justify with logic.

Your look and feel should be intentional, consistent, and reflective of the results you deliver.

The quality of your pixels and every aspect of your design should be clean and precise.

Everything should be done on purpose, not by accident.

Key Brand Elements:

- Color Palette – Choose 2–3 core colors that evoke emotion and reflect your brand's mood.

- Typography – Use clean, readable fonts that match your brand voice (e.g., bold, elegant, modern).

- Photography & Videography – Select images that align with your lifestyle, personality, and offer. Pixels clear & clean.

- Logo & Name – Keep it simple and memorable across all digital platforms.

- Message – What thoughts are provoked by what you say, stand for, and how you say it? What tone do you consistently carry?

Speaker Pro Tip: Build a visual identity board to clarify and lock in your brand's look and message tone. This also makes it easy for staff & contractors who design for you to have a clear vision of their guidelines.

Your Notes:

_____
_____
_____
_____
_____

Section 3: Build Emotional Connection Through Brand Energy

People connect with spirit before they connect with expertise.

Your brand should make your audience feel something... seen, empowered, inspired, or challenged.

Ask & write out:

- How do people feel after experiencing my content?
- Is my brand making a meaningful impression?
- Am I creating an emotional connection... or just aesthetics?
- Does my audience feel the emotional connection is genuine or "put on"?

Branding isn't about being fancy. It's about being unforgettable...

Preferably, in a good way.

I'm going to say something here that you may not have heard before... but you know me – I'm the truth teller. People will stereotype you by your look. YUP... they will judge the quality of your clothing, the content of your character and your class level by it. Don't let this be a negative take away though.

Knowing this allows you to choose who you want to show up as and more importantly who you want to attract to your world. Your highest paying engagements will many times come from people/organizations who also align with how you present your personal style to the world.

In our company, we go as far as to do avatar trainings, personality tests and mood boards. We may release them to the public soon, make sure to sign up for our email list at www.thespeakerpreneur.com and register for the email list. For now... make a mood board of your favorite looks that align with your personality and character.

Make a decision that you will always show up/brand yourself in a way that is true to who you are, which is ultimately who you want in your world. Whether that is jeans and a t-shirt, a flashy suit, bold color blocking, elegance and simplicity, afro-centric, or other... choosing time and place is key. We don't change who we are to get into a space to speak... that causes an identity crisis— we choose the worlds we align with and partner with those. So, budget your attire in your expenses. It can also be counted towards uniform cost in tax prep.

Section 4: Be Consistent Everywhere

We've mentioned before... consistency & congruency builds credibility. The same is true here.

From your social media bios to your website to your podcast intro (if applicable), your brand should look and sound like the same person everywhere.

Audit Checklist:

- Does my Instagram bio match my LinkedIn headline?
- Do my photos, messaging, and colors align?
- Is my brand voice clear and consistent in videos, captions, and content?
    - Other social media outlets of mine representing this same brand?
- Do my funnels carry the same message and color scheme across all pages, or am I confusing people with too many mixed messages, brand elements, or offers?

Financially independent speakerpreneur brands are recognizable and repeatable. People should be able to describe you in one sentence because your brand positioning is so clear. Place your notes below.

_____

_____

_____

_____

_____

_____

_____

_____

_____

Section 5: Align With Your Future Self

Don't just build your brand from your current situation... build it from the vision you're walking into, and work your way into the now should you need to.

Ask and write out:

- How does the next-level version of me show up?
- What kind of brand would attract premium opportunities?
- Would someone earning 7-figures, 8-figures, or 9 figures show up this way? (use your goal)

When you design from your future self, you attract opportunities that match your new level as your body walks through the current level.

Your Notes:

_____

_____

_____

_____

_____

_____

_____

_____

_____

_____

_____

_____

_____

_____

_____

Conclusion: Brand With Intention, Lead With Love, Purpose & Influence

Your brand is your billboard, your business card, and your silent salesperson.

When built with clarity, strategy, and purpose, it positions you as the go-to authority in your industry.

Not only that, but you unequivocally demonstrate and embody it in a way that shifts a room and screams authenticity. This is building a brand from the inside out.

I can't tell you how many speakerpreneurs are lost, broken, alone, and threatened to give up because they are out of alignment with these principles.

On the other hand, I can't tell you how many people think they are zoned in on purpose, but they are missing the "humph" in their process.

When you are truly aligned with purpose and expose that purpose in excellent brand form, profits MUST naturally bow and follow.

It's just common sense & it happens every time it's done well.

You're not just creating content...
you're creating a legacy.

Be seen, be strategic, and let your brand speak of success before you say a word.

In the next step, we'll explore how to package your message into products that scale your brand and serve your audience at every level.

For Now... It's Reflection time.

REFLECTION & ACTION TIME

Use this time to reflect over your notes, pray/meditate and make a plan of action from this step accordingly. Use an additional notebook if necessary, add dates and times to carry out the mission.

Goal | (Event that has Occurred in the spirit realm).

What is the specific goal or milestone you're focusing on right now?

_____

_____

_____

Steps Leading to the Goal

Break down the steps you need to take to reach this goal, one by one.

_____

_____

_____

Potential Obstacles

What might get in the way of you completing these steps?

_____

_____

_____

Support System

Who or what can help you overcome these obstacles or keep them manageable?

_____

_____

_____

STEP 8: PRODUCT CREATION – BUILDING YOUR WEALTH LADDER

Introduction: Your Products Are Your Path to Scalable Income

One of the most powerful ways to increase your impact and income as a speakerpreneur is by turning your knowledge into products and services.

Products particularly create leverage.

They allow you to serve many, even when you're not in the room.

Financially independent speakerpreneurs don't rely on one stream of income—they create what I call... product/service ecosystems.

This = diversified income.

From entry-level digital downloads to high-end coaching containers, your products should guide your audience up a value ladder that delivers transformation at every level.

These are not just random AI thrown together products either.

These are carefully crafted result-based pieces of work that will change the world through your methods... AND they don't have to take a long time to create.

This step will help you strategically design, position, and launch products that multiply your message and your money.

If you do not have products, take this time to release product ideas below.

_____

_____

_____

_____

_____

_____

_____

Section 1: Understand the Product Ecosystem

You don't need a hundred offers.

You need a clear pathway.

Think of your product suite as a ladder (we mentioned this before remember):

- **Low-ticket**: $27–$197+ (books, PDFs, workbooks, digital downloads)

- **Mid-ticket**: $297–$997+ (courses, challenges, group programs)

- **High-ticket**: $1,500+ (coaching, consulting, masterminds, retreats)

- **Premium or B2b high level**: ($10K+)

Each product should:

- Solve a specific problem/symptom
- Lead into the next level of transformation
- Align with your signature message

People have often asked me why I don't include "free" as an offer when I teach this.

It has nothing to do with me not believing in free products, opt-ins, giveaways, etc. It has everything to do with the fact that, at this moment in time, I believe society has been conditioned to give things away for free... as a way of offering trash to the audience for their own personal gain.

I don't believe in giving trash to an audience. And if I'm not giving trash, the only thing I'll be giving for free is what I truly feel led by God to give.

I remember many years ago, a mentor once told me to give away things I love to the poor... items I would still consider worthy of wearing myself at that time in my life. The way I see it, that same principle applies in business.

The value of a freebie is very subjective based on the offer, the community, or the niche you're in. Make sure free makes sense when and if you give it.

If you attend one of our training sessions, you may hear me tell one person to give something away for free, while advising someone else in a different niche to only offer a low-ticket product—discouraging a freebie altogether.

That said, I do tend to recommend free webinars to the majority of niches and audiences, because they are one of the highest-quality freebies you can offer… and if done well, the return is still strong.

You may also hear me advise offering a freebie with a purchase often.

Just know this: with everything being stated here, free should never equal trash.

Anything you give away for free should still hold high value and have the power to shift the tone or result for the person who trusted you enough to download it or spend time reading it.

Give at your best, never at your worst, for you will reap exactly what you sow & sell. Here's a note space below for your thoughts and planning.

_____

_____

_____

_____

_____

_____

_____

_____

_____

_____

_____

_____

_____

Section 2: Start With What You Already Know

You don't need to reinvent yourself - unless you had or are having an identity crisis, or you are creating a complete shift in your life.

Your first product can come from what you've already done, experienced, or taught in your zone of genius. It has to be something people truly want to buy... not something you're forcing on them.

This is where product market fit matters and BOYYYYY does it matter...

Product-Market Fit (PMF) – a critical concept in entrepreneurship and marketing that refers to the point at which a product satisfies strong market demand. It's the moment when your product solves a real problem for a specific group of people—and they're willing to pay for it, recommend it, and keep using it.

If they won't pay for it in droves... you won't have a thriving company.

Ask yourself:

- What do people always ask me for that I deliver top-tier results in?
- What transformations have I already helped someone tangibly achieve?
- What process do I repeat that could be packaged?
- What are they really buying from me — in their eyes — that they need right now?

Speaker Pro tip:

Document what you know.

Systematize your expertise.

Turn your methods into modules or steps. The formula rules.

Remember, brain dumping gets those formulas out.

These questions above are meant for brain dumping and processing.

Just because people ask you to provide something doesn't mean that's necessarily what you should be serving.

All of these questions are for you to write down and consider.

Here's a vital point to process as you come up to your next notes and planning section.

Remember your products and services should be in direct alignment with your speaking topic/niche. They all work together hand in hand.

You should not be an expert on gut health, have a product/service on gut health and then speak on romance after trauma. Unless, your audience is already highly aware that if they fix their gut health, it will directly cure the issues they are struggling with in the romance after trauma arena.

Keep in mind as well, should you go that lane, you'd be pressed to prove that case VERY well… like undeniably well, or your audience is then confused and will not buy in bulk services and products from you. Everything should be cohesive. You've got this.

I promise, if you're doing every step in this book, the notes in front of you will scream change and cash loudly in your face.

Section 3: Low-Ticket Products – Build Authority and Audience

Low-ticket products are perfect for lead generation and credibility building. They're generally faster to create (once your teaching framework is built out), easy to sell, and great for giving your audience a taste of your work. Of course, because you've aligned it with a true NEED in your marketplace... the need you provide the solution to.

You must also make sure the message is SUPER clear.

A few low ticket product formats:

- Mini-course or digital workshop
- eBook or audio training
- Script bundle or templates
- PDF
- Webinar

These products should deliver a quick win.

Keep it focused.

One problem.

One solution.

This will generally be one or two steps pulled from your full-fledged system or product that gives a high-level, but effective approach.

Release the low ticket products you've made a decision to execute below.

_____

_____

_____

_____

_____

Section 4: Mid-Ticket Offers – Deliver Results at Scale...

Mid-ticket products usually help you serve many without sacrificing your time.

They're perfect for community-based transformation and scalable growth.

Possible Format Examples:

- 6-week live group coaching program
- On-demand course with structured content
- Guided challenge or bootcamp

Framework:

- Clear start and end
- Defined outcome
- Modules, Q&A, support community (optional)

This is the zone where your business starts gaining serious momentum.

Your Notes:

_____

_____

_____

_____

_____

_____

_____

_____

_____

Section 5: High-Ticket Offers – Premium Transformation, Premium Profit

This is where your deepest value lives.

Most times, your high-ticket offer is for people who want direct access to you, accelerated results, and elevated experiences.

Examples:

- One-on-one coaching or consulting package
- VIP strategy days (virtual or in-person)
- Mastermind, retreat, workshop

High-Ticket Tips:

- Solve a high-stakes problem with some Done-For-You (DFY) or DFY-like options.
- Offer a personalized, high-touch experience.
- Position it with premium branding and strong results.
- Remember, high-ticket prices come from high-ticket problems—don't just throw around high-ticket pricing. Pricing should be meaningful and well thought out, not just a sticker.

Don't price from fear or scarcity… Price from value and outcome.

I personally run my prices through what I call the "God filter," beyond just technical knowledge.

- Lord, is this what I should be charging for this service tier?
- Is this price aligned with the lifestyle you desire for me?
- Is this the right price, for right now?
- Help me see where my prices should stay and grow this season, Lord.
- Show me my intentions in pricing this way.

- Father, help me not to settle when I know I am called to harvest the riches of this land. I've made the decision to do so, and my pricing reflects that.

From a technical pricing standpoint, I advise considering, but not being limited to the following questions:

- What is the going rate in my field for this product/service?
- What is my current financial situation, and what do I need to make right now?
- Is there an amount I'm willing to settle for temporarily? How long?
- What does my belief system say I have the confidence to achieve at this moment?
- What is the highest ticket I believe (or want to believe) I can sell right now?
- Does this price make sense for my avatar to pay?
- What is the cost to deliver this service versus what I am charging?
- Is my attitude negatively affected by charging this price? Why?
- How much marketing budget do I have to spend to get people to buy this product/service?

Pricing is strategic.

Poor pricing decisions can damage a business financially.

Many fail at this, costing even the best businesses their livelihood. So, consider it carefully.

Listen to the Spirit of God and work with the knowledge you have.

Remove excess emotion around pricing.

Feel free to attend our local events for live, in-person help.

We host private sessions throughout the year designed to help with this and more. Visit **www.thespeakerpreneur.com** and register as you implement the steps here in the guide.

Section 6: Package With Simplicity and Precision

Full-time speakerpreneurs build products that are not cluttered, they are clear.

Your product descriptions, pricing, and outcomes must be instantly understandable.

Checklist:

- Who is this for?

- What straight-down-the-middle problem does it solve?

- What result can they expect?

- How long is it?

- What's included?

- How do they buy it?

The clearer and simpler you are, the faster they buy.

Write your answers to these questions and keep them close… along with everything else from this guide.

Your Notes:

_____

_____

_____

_____

_____

_____

_____

_____

_____

Conclusion: Multi Paid speaking is where the CASH is...

Products and services help you achieve what I call multi-paid speaking.

Many of you may have heard me teach this before, whether I've been in your city, you've attended one of my free workshops, or other...

You may have heard one of my more popular students, mentees, or an event attendee speak on it.

The basics are simple:

Before the stage: You receive your deposit (minimum 50% non-refundable). You can also structure deals where they purchase your products along with your speaking deposit.

During the stage: Before or during the client pays your remaining balance, and you're also able to sell your products and services from the stage.

After the stage: Your products and services continue to sell from the impact you made on the room. As you share how people can stay connected and purchase from you, they enter your world. And you connect for more engagements from that room at the establishment and beyond.

Btw... I call that product piece in "after the stage"... the gift that keeps on giving.

Long after you've exited the room, the impact remains and your income continues. That same audience is now a part of your ecosystem.

For a bit of a deeper entail on the connection piece I spoke of... You are also asking the booking agent if they have any additional engagements that match your skill set, and whether they have referrals they believe you would collaborate well with.

This goes deeper, but these elements are the most important basics.

We'll tackle more of that when I see you at an event... online or in person.

Overall...

You are sitting on profitable content.

Your frameworks, life experiences, and strategies are worth packaging.

As you now fully understand, products allow you to scale your genius and build a business that works even after you've stepped off the stage.

The remnants of what you've done on stage add up.

Design your product suite with intention.

Build for your audience's journey.

Price for impact and profit.

In the next step, we'll dive into how to craft your signature speech... the story and strategy that will open doors, close deals, and position you as a sought-after expert.

Repeater:

- Free/Low Ticket ($0–$197+): eBooks, PDFs, workshops, digital templates
- Mid Ticket ($297–$997+): Group programs, live intensives, self-paced courses
- High Ticket ($1,500+): Private coaching, VIP sessions, done-for-you services, masterminds
- Premium or B2B High-Level ($10K+): Advanced consulting, corporate contracts, licensing, premium retainers

This is just for guidance. You'll need to research your world & industry prices for better accuracy.

Last note for this section.

Some might ask "Coach Court, if I have a million products and services, which should I pitch from the stage?"

That answer is simple. The one(s) that matches the ultimate need of those in the room. That's why you don't need tons of products and services to begin this journey. You may never have more than 2-20 products etc. It doesn't matter. You can be full time, make impressive impact and be very well off financially with just one product & one service... or even a few products and a few services.

More on stage pitching later.

For now... It's Reflection time.

REFLECTION & ACTION TIME

Use this time to reflect over your notes, pray/meditate and make a plan of action from this step accordingly. Use an additional notebook if necessary, add dates and times to carry out the mission.

Goal | (Event that has Occurred in the spirit realm).

What is the specific goal or milestone you're focusing on right now?

_____

_____

_____

Steps Leading to the Goal

Break down the steps you need to take to reach this goal, one by one.

_____

_____

_____

Potential Obstacles

What might get in the way of you completing these steps?

_____

_____

_____

Support System

Who or what can help you overcome these obstacles or keep them manageable?

_____

_____

_____

STEP 9: THE SIGNATURE SPEECH – SHARING YOUR STORY, SHIFTING THE ROOM

Introduction: Your Voice Is Your Most Valuable Asset

Your story, your insight, your conviction and your expertise are the keys to creating connection and commanding rooms.

Your signature speech is not just a talk or a testimony, it's a transformational message that activates, inspires, and positions you as a vessel of impact & cash flow.

It's also a seed planted and for some harvested right then and there.

Like John you are the voice crying in the wilderness, but like Solomon, David, Job & Peter you are a skilled business owner.

Whether you're on stage, hosting a webinar, or leading a workshop, your signature speech should not only move people emotionally… it should also guide them strategically to take action on a physical journey of transformation.

This step will help you write and deliver a powerful, story & offer based message that resonates and creates opportunity.

Section 1: Understand the Purpose of the Speech (pitch and presentation)

Your speech isn't just content—it's a catalyst. It should:

- Tell your story with purpose and intention
- Position your offer as the next step with irrefutable proof
- Shift, Solidify and/or Confirm the mindset of your audience
- Invite & Ignite transformation and action

A great speech — presentation, and pitch create momentum.

It turns listeners into buyers, followers into believers, and stages into platforms for expansion.

Think about the story you want to tell and how it aligns with your products/services.

_____

_____

_____

_____

_____

_____

_____

_____

_____

_____

_____

_____

_____

_____

Section 2: Choose the Right Story

The most powerful speeches are rooted in truth and transformation.

Your story doesn't have to be dramatic — but it does need to be authentic.

It also needs to match the room. Every story is NOT for every room.

The story part of your speech is typically used in the presentation, but you can weave elements of it into your pitch to remind the audience how a specific part of your offer is helpful.

Remember: the stories of others are also very relevant to both your presentation and pitch.

Stories can be used as: 1. Point solidifiers 2. Testimonials 3. Truth and facts to support the case you're making - (these are just a top few)

You are appealing to the subconscious jury of your audience's mind every time you give a speech.

Present your case, provide evidence, and appeal to the jury with care...

And make sure you've chosen the right jury (avatar) to present to.

To choose the right story for the room, ask:

- What defining moments shifted my perspective or unlocked my purpose for this particular forum? (Same if you're sharing someone else's story.)

- What have I walked through that prepared me to lead others to the solution needed here? (Same if you're telling another's story.)

- What breakthrough did I experience that my audience is hungry for right now... today? (Same if sharing someone else's breakthrough.)

Let your story or stories be specific, heartfelt, and anchored in a lesson that matters.

No rambling... unless it's a tactic that grabs your audience at their core.

There's only one rule: grab them by the stomach, pluck their heartstrings, and infuse them with a new beginning or a new level of greatness.

Section 3: Structure Your Signature Talk for Impact

Use this basic proven speech framework to start out :

1. **The Hook** (Intro)– Open with something that grabs attention, but make sure it matters to the reason they came into the room today, specifically to hear your talk. (I never recommend starting with an about me section, but that's just my tactic. The way I see it, they care more about why they're there than who we are—in most cases.)

2. **The Room Confirmation** (Intro)–Make sure they understand they're in the right room. Reiterate what will be discussed and what they'll walk away with if they stay tuned.

3. **The Struggle & the Mindset of the Solution** (Content) – Address the core issue they're dealing with and the struggles surrounding it. Share your personal turning point or challenge, or the turning point/challenge of a relevant story character. This is where you introduce your framework, process, or strategy. Add irrefutable proof.

4. **The Shift** (Transition) – Reveal what changed and the insight gained. Don't forget to show the proof and evidence that backs up the transformation. Now, remind them how this affects their bottom line and will shift their issue as well.

5. **The Invitation** (Offer, Close, Q&A) – Naturally transition into your offer or call to action. Be clear and descriptive about your process. Deliver your closing remarks, then open the floor for Q&A.

Every part of your speech should lead your audience from inspiration to activation.

I have several tips and tricks to convert speech frameworks—literally thousands. I could go on at this all day, but for now, this will help you immensely!

I've coached vets in the speaking game that were still missing these elements... once added their whole speech transformed and their cash shot up. It's your turn.

As always, feel free to attend an event near you when I speak, so I can break it down even more.

I look forward to meeting you—in person or virtually.

Visit: www.thespeakerpreneur.com to register for upcoming events.

Section 4: Align the Story and the Message With the Market

Make sure your story connects directly to your ideal client's journey.

Ask and write down:

- Does this story illustrate a result they want?
- Is the takeaway practical and relevant?
- Does my talk position my offer as the solution?

Be sure to include:

- Language your audience uses (mirror their thoughts and words)
- Clear, relatable examples
- Answers to their objections
- Opportunities for the person to consciously and subconsciously agree with your statements.
- A closing that plants and waters a seed of transformation. Throw some nature-grown fertilizer on that "thang" too. Make the offer.

Moral Compass Reminder: It's a privilege and honor to influence a mind. People are trusting you with their attention, be cautious of how you use that power.

Your Notes:

_____

_____

_____

_____

_____

Section 5: Rehearse With Intention, Energy and Excellence

Confidence isn't just spiritual... it's practiced.

High level speakers rehearse so they can release their message with power, structure, and flow at the same time.

A lot is going on when you speak.

One of the biggest problems I've seen with many speakers, especially those who happen to be of Christian origin, is that they forsake structure for flow.

I believe vice versa is neither correct.

God is both order and flow.

In essence... the order is a part of the flow.

You must manage the voice of God alongside your technical skills at the same time.

When speaking, you're managing...

- God / Spirit

- The room / audience

- Your knowledge + wisdom

That's why this skill is so powerful when matched with your supernatural power.

Geesh, I'm getting hot just talking about it.

"I done' wrote myself happy."

Your Notes:

_____

_____

_____

_____

Practice tips:

- Record and review yourself fully clothed—just like you would on the actual event day.
- Practice in front of peers or mentors.
- Time each section to ensure good pacing and focus on memorizing key points, not necessarily every single word.
- Pray, prepare, and get present before you speak.
- Practice as if you're in front of your specific audience—imagine their reactions, not just any audience.
- Practice in your imagination, not just physically.

When your message is memorized, or at least embedded in your heart, spirit & mind... you speak from overflow, not anxiety.

Your Notes:

_____
_____
_____
_____
_____
_____
_____
_____
_____
_____
_____
_____

Section 6: Let the Speech Do the Selling

The strongest speeches don't randomly "sell"... they *serve* so well that the offer & the sell become the next logical step.

Again, they confirm or deny suspicions. This is why there is nothing wrong with sales.

In fact, it's your MORAL DUTY to sell, so lives can be transformed... if you're called to business.

The hefty sales portion in the speech generally comes at the end. Although prep for it is throughout.

There are ways to sell books, opt-ins, etc., in between though... It's just more complicated... more advanced.

I would not advise it to a newbie, but if you're confident... go for it. I say work up to that and stay focused on just one pitch at a time.

For the ending pitch... I advise you to stack your transitions. Some people would only use one of these key elements below.

I use them all, but I word them differently. See these as a guide placed together in bulk at one time...

A few seamless ways to transition:

- I've shown you this today...

- The only reason you are in this position needing help is because...

- "I know this message spoke to some of you and you're ready for more...

- "That's exactly why I created [insert offer name]..."

- "Let me walk you through how this becomes your reality and answer questions you may have after

If I'm pitching at the end of my speech, I stack the benefits of my offer one at a time, reiterating the previous ones as I go.

Then I present the bonuses with less explanation.

After that, I share pricing and next steps. The goal is to create alignment between your story, your teaching, and your solution.

Conclusion: Speak to Shift the Atmosphere

You are not just a speaker... you are a messenger.

Your signature speech is the vehicle God will use to impact lives, open doors, and expand your platform. Speak with clarity. Share with authority. Offer with intention & power. Sell with structure and humility.

In the next step, we'll break down how to attract and direct traffic to your message and offers—using both organic and paid strategies to expand your influence. As we go into reflection time here a few hefty last notes to help more with speech conversion and remind you of important keys from this section.

1 - Remember you are presenting to what I call the audience's subconscious jury in their mind. You must state your facts and prove them with evidence.

2 - Make sure that your presentation creates an atmosphere through your tone, your passion, the slides presented if they are presented, your body language which will sometimes also replace the slides and your SKILLSET being incorporated.

3 - Your authority in your craft must speak. Put some RESPECT on your name.

When you are pitching you offer start with key components then go into bonuses. Let your client results - through your stories with teaching examples - show these components and benefits. As you list your bonuses, list them in order of what they truly need to succeed in your process. Every time you list one - recap the one prior until they are all done. Then, state your price and what you have done to make the price convenient for them. Once price is revealed you will state a CRAAAAZZYYYY last bonus that they get if they take advantage of this offer today and then you will take questions. A website link on screen, or qr code is needed for them to take advantage of the offer right away.

If you are on a stage where you can do a full pitch... do it at ALL times. Do not be scared to pitch. People need what you have right?

If you are on a stage where you can not do a full pitch, try pitching socials. Invite them to dm (direct message), or pm (private message) you a specific word to get them started "use language that aligns with your soul" and the offer. If they can meet you at the event right after your speech that is even better. Have them stand in line and book them in right away for a call (or other offer) at the event. Staff is preferred to help with this, but you can start alone if needed. The sooner they make a commitment. The better. If you register them for a sales call, I would advise having a replay of that event or one of your other teaching events, so they can remember the experience that led them to you in the first place.

Now It's Reflection time.

REFLECTION & ACTION TIME

Use this time to reflect over your notes, pray/meditate and make a plan of action from this step accordingly. Use an additional notebook if necessary, add dates and times to carry out the mission.

Goal | (Event that has Occurred in the spirit realm).

What is the specific goal or milestone you're focusing on right now?

_____

_____

_____

Steps Leading to the Goal

Break down the steps you need to take to reach this goal, one by one.

_____

_____

_____

Potential Obstacles

What might get in the way of you completing these steps?

_____

_____

_____

Support System

Who or what can help you overcome these obstacles or keep them manageable?

_____

_____

_____

STEP 10: TRAFFIC & LEAD MAGNETS – BRINGING PEOPLE INTO YOUR WORLD

Introduction: Visibility is a Vehicle for Purpose & of Course, Finance

Like any other business or offer…

You can have the most powerful message, a transformative offer, and an anointed brand—but if no one knows you exist, you can't fulfill your assignment at scale.

Visibility isn't vanity… it's stewardship.

It's about showing up consistently so the people you're called to serve can find you.

Recall when God declared to Abraham… "I will make your name famous".

Popularity is not poison; it's positioning.

In the digital world, "traffic" refers to the people visiting your content, landing pages, and social profiles.

It's what brings people to the top of your funnel, where connection begins.

In the same manner, you should adapt this mindset in your speaking. Yes, it's (one and the same/the same).

Think of traffic (web traffic, social media attention, podcast interviews, etc.) as the top of your opportunity funnel.

The more eyeballs you get in front of the right people, the more likely event planners, organizers, and corporate buyers will discover you.

And every piece of content is a speaker audition.

One of the main things I love to teach speakers is to utilize "talking" social media content to drive traffic to their pages through paid and organic advertising.

This helps to build your audience around your gift of speaking, which puts you at top of mind for gigs vs only capitalizing from still content or talking content that is not in your speaking/teaching zone of interest.

Your job isn't to "chase" people—it's to attract their attention- grab them and hold that attention with clarity, value, and authenticity… And then earn the right to go after them. This step shows you how to use both organic and paid traffic strategies to build momentum and grow your mission.

Section 1: Understand the Purpose of Traffic

Traffic is about exposure. Exposure to the right people is the key.

Your job is to make sure that you call the right people in your advertising messages and select the right people in whatever paid marketing tools you are using.

You're planting seeds - yes... but you're also inviting them to stay and grow as they come.

The more people who encounter your content - which consists of your stories and offers, the more hearts you can impact.

Let me be clear.

One of the amazing parts of creating awesome presentations and pitches – in the way you're learning through this guide - is that you've already done the work needed to create millions of content pieces.

Creating your signature speech and pitch is like soaking a thick towel in a bucket of water.

The water = everything you've lived, learned, overcome, and mastered. Your accumulated wisdom, mistakes, breakthroughs, research, and lessons.

You soak the towel in that. It's heavy and wet... filled with water! The towel—that's your speech.

The deep work of building your core message is right there: your story, your framework, your transformation promise.

You pour your best ideas, experience, and value into one concentrated source—fully saturated with clarity, conviction, and cash-generating potential.

Here's where the blessing happens: you don't toss the towel after one use.

You wring it out—strategically, consistently, and creatively.

You wring it out—over and over again.

Each twist of that towel becomes:

- A reel or video clip

- A podcast episode
- An email sequence
- A landing page or freebie
- A book or book chapter
- A course lesson
- A sales page or webinar
- A pitch to a new client, sponsor, or brand

You're extracting dozens, hundreds, even millions of assets from that one saturated speech.

Get it?

Now you can see it more right?

It's awesome & reclaims your time.

Always remember, you need *consistent* traffic...

- It fills your funnel with aligned prospects
- It gives more people access to your message

And your speech is the sidekick to present to that traffic.

Let's get something clear about the traffic mindset...

You're not showing up just to go viral... you're showing up to ruffle feathers, stand on business, and stand on purpose.

That's a huge part of what creates virality.

You're showing up to be obedient, consistent, and excellent in your calling.

Sales and bookings come from that kind of showing up—if you have the right system... And you're learning the keys to that now.

Remember, traffic is not the same as leads until they've shown interest in your product or service.

This is where effective CTA's come in...

The clear invitation you give that guides your audience toward their next decision.

For now, new traffic acts as potential prospects and if you and/or your team did your job right... they become good ones.

What type of traffic are you consciously or unconsciously using right now? How is it working? Here's some note space below.

_____

_____

_____

_____

_____

_____

_____

On a side note: Just to drop a bit more with social media, since we mentioned it again.

Below, are the few beginner elements I'd say every speakerpreneur should have for their social media and use accordingly. Please google these if you are not familiar with them, or feel free to contact us at www.thespeakerpreneur.com to get more help in creating/understanding these elements.

Key Content Templates to have on deck:

Ig story series graphics, Fb banner graphics, Ig talking head cover decals, "Speaking in your city" graphic (both square & Ig Story), Launch graphic (both square & Ig Story), Fb Banners with event announcements (square fb post & ig story size), Event & Book/Product announcement graphics (great for anthologies – fb & ig reel size), Eventbrite cover graphic, Program launch graphic (both ig story & fb size), twitter quote graphic (ig reel, ig square & fb square size)

You may also interchangeably use Ig story graphic sizes as reels and your fb square graphic size should be able to cross between many other platforms.

It may also be good to have email headers with each of these as well. Now let's get back to traffic.

Section 2: Organic Traffic – Build Trust Through Consistency

Organic traffic is free and built through content. It's slower and more inconsistent in growth generally than paid methods, but it still usually builds deep trust when used well consistently. That's the key to organic... the right message accompanied by consistency.

I personally don't believe in staying only organic in 99.9% of businesses. I advise that if you are organic right now, run to mix your organic with paid strategies.

It will save you time and energy.

A few organic strategies include:

- Free Social media content (Instagram, Facebook, LinkedIn, YouTube, etc.)

- Free Podcasts and interviews

- Free Guest features or blog posts

- Free Email newsletters

- Free Live streaming and workshops

- Other free outside speaking engagements & events in front of a group of aligned people

Keys to Success for Organic Traffic:

- Consistency... I'd recommend posting 3–5x/week minimum if you're currently relying on organic methods.

- Using socials? Make sure you have a mix of offers—include your speaking offers, face-forward teaching content, demonstration content showcasing your expertise, transformation receipts/results, and day-in-the-life content.

- Provide high-value insights tied to your message and offer. People should say, "This person is my encyclopedia for this world. I can find everything here on this specific topic."

- Use strong hooks, stories, and calls-to-action.

Organic visibility is about being present, immensely valuable, and relatable.

Section 3: Paid Traffic – Accelerate Exposure With Strategy

Paid traffic uses money to speed up reach.

If you have a clear offer and message, ads can help you reach hundreds, thousands & millions + of new potential leads faster.

Especially if you are already making consistent sales from your offer.

A few Popular Paid traffic channels right now:

- Meta (Facebook & Instagram) ads (many social media platforms these days are now offering ads as well. In the future I predict they all will.)

- YouTube ads

- Google Search ads

- Sponsored posts or collaborations

- Paid speaking engagements/events

- Paid high-quality speaking engagements

Tips:

- Almost every organic method can turn into a paid method.

- Start with a low daily budget if needed (e.g., $5–10). I say there's never a time not to run ads—except if you have $0 and no message. Seek guidance with this. Not every tactic works with low ad spend.

- Direct ads to a high-value lead magnet. This is a tactic we use with our clients for low-ticket ads, and it generally gives us the highest conversions—especially event-based lead magnets.

- Test different headlines, videos, and messages. Ads are not an overnight process. You may need to test many versions before finding the right starters. Ads are ongoing. You will continue to create and test for the life of your business… get used to this.

Remember once more: Paid ads are most effective when your message, audience, and funnel are already dialed in.

Just the basics.

Many people spend a lot of money on ads, but are missing key pieces of the funnel.

A funnel is the journey someone takes from first discovering you to eventually hiring you, buying from you, or working with you.

When evaluating why your ads aren't working, consider your offer, message, ad targeting, and sales process.

We run exposure ads for speaking engagements and conversion ads for other products and services.

Ads can be tricky—but they're worth it.

You don't have a business that scales without consistent eyeballs to convert and conversations to be had.

If you're someone who wants to dive even deeper into this and you're more hands-on…

We can teach you more.

Look for our upcoming in-person or virtual events to get the support you need.

Go to **www.thespeakerpreneur.com** for event dates & more resources.

_____

_____

_____

_____

_____

_____

_____

_____

_____

_____

Section 4: Lead Magnets – Give First, Grow Fast

In our world... A lead magnet is a resource you give in exchange for a potential buyer's email address &/or attention, generally free or low-ticket.

It positions you as an expert, provides value upfront, and begins the relationship.

A great lead magnet will also light a fire of desire for your ideal client to see exactly why they should spend their money with you.

It should handle objections.

A few types of lead magnets include:

- Free or low-ticket checklist or workbook

- 1 day or multi-day event... things like mindset challenges go in that realm as well

- Mini training/course or video series

- A quiz that helps your audience identify their stage or struggle

Speaker Tip: Serve before you sell.

Earn their attention and their sell.

Focus on real transformation, even in your free or low-ticket content.

Your lead magnet should:

- Solve a specific symptom, not just a pain point or desire.

- Be delivered instantly... don't make them wait forever for what they got

- Lead into your paid offer seamlessly... upsell options should always be available if they need it.

Section 5: Follow-Up That Nurtures and Converts

Once someone downloads or signs up for your lead magnet, don't drop the ball.

It's good ethics & your job to keep the connection alive.

One way to do so... Use email to serve, share, and invite them to go deeper.

Email sequences allow you to nurture your audience over time— building connection, credibility, and trust without having to be present 24/7.

They do require intentional buildout and testing for conversion.

It's not a one-shot deal... but absolutely worth getting right.

Your sequence gives you space to:

- Share your story
- Explain your unique method or framework
- Overcome objections
- Showcase results and testimonials
- Paint the picture of what life could look like after working with you

Here are a few things to remember when creating an email sequence around this:

- Email 1: Deliver the freebie + welcome them to your world
- Email 2: Share elements of your story or a "day in the life," keeping the focus on why they signed up in the first place. Link them to another part of your world for more value.
- Email 3: Provide a win or tip related to the lead magnet.
- Email 4: Introduce (or reintroduce) your offer.
- Email 5: Share testimonials or case studies in a "juicy" format.
- Email 6: Invite them to take the next step with urgency and scarcity.

My advice...

Let your emails sound like a conversation, not a sales pitch - until it's time for that.

Speak with intention, authority, and care.

It's important to note that email is nothing without traffic.

I mean... who are you sending emails to?

At some point, you will exhaust that audience & if you are only selling to them every minute, you will exhaust them faster than the speed of light.

There is nothing wrong with a strong pitch once you've clarified the need for it.

Plan your email sequence here.

_____

_____

_____

_____

_____

_____

_____

_____

_____

_____

_____

_____

_____

Conclusion: Let Them Find You Prepared

Your visibility is not about striving... it's about serving.

When you show up consistently and intentionally with faith, value, and strategy, you position yourself to be discovered by the people you're meant to help.

Lead with undeniable truths.

Attract with authenticity.

Again... build with intention.

Pitch with passion and authority.

In the next step, we'll walk through how to design a soul-aligned sales process that honors both your clients and your calling.

For now... It's Reflection Time again.

If you're bombarded with ideas and thoughts, feel free to write them here before you get into reflection time.

_____

_____

_____

_____

_____

_____

_____

_____

_____

_____

REFLECTION & ACTION TIME

Use this time to reflect over your notes, pray/meditate and make a plan of action from this step accordingly. Use an additional notebook if necessary, add dates and times to carry out the mission.

Goal | (Event that has Occurred in the spirit realm).

What is the specific goal or milestone you're focusing on right now?

_____

_____

_____

Steps Leading to the Goal

Break down the steps you need to take to reach this goal, one by one.

_____

_____

_____

Potential Obstacles

What might get in the way of you completing these steps?

_____

_____

_____

Support System

Who or what can help you overcome these obstacles or keep them manageable?

_____

_____

_____

STEP 11: SALES PROCESS – GUIDING YOUR AUDIENCE TO SAY YES WITH CONFIDENCE

Introduction: Selling is Serving

Let's bring back this reminder...

Sales isn't about convincing people... it's about clearly inviting them into a solution you've been anointed to provide & confirming the suspicions they already had as a truth.

When you shift your mindset from "selling" to "serving with intention," everything changes. Your sales process becomes an act of integrity, not pressure.

In sales, you are never pushing your services on people. Some of you may have heard the saying...

"Anyone who provides a service to someone is a doctor within their niche."

I genuinely agree. In fact, this is one thing most marketers genuinely agree on.

Every prospective client you are targeting NEEDS your service. Like a patient NEEDS a doctor, they need healing, and you are genuinely providing that healing through your solution to their problem.

You are not selling for money, you are selling to help. That help has money attached to it... if you ask for it.

By the end of your doctor visit, the doctor tells you, "Ok, this is the plan of action, and this is the amount it will cost to do so."

You don't complain. You get ready to pay, and you thank the doctor for taking the time to help you.

The same should be true for your service.

The reason your prospect has chosen to see you — the expert — is because they genuinely have a problem, and something in them believes you genuinely have a solution.

Financially independent speakerpreneurs who are faith-driven, like myself, understand that sales is ministry. You're helping someone step into a better version of themselves — spiritually, emotionally, financially, or relationally.

This step will show you how to create a sales process that is both heart-centered and effective.

For me personally... it is also Holy Spirit–led.

Section 1: What is a Sales/Funnel Process?

A sales process is the step-by-step journey someone takes from discovering you to investing in your offer.

Typical stages:

1. Awareness (they discover your content or message)
2. Interest (they review & engage with your content)
3. Connection typically goes along with interest (they feel seen, heard, and understood)
4. Invitation (you offer the next step Examples: call, email, or webinar)
5. Decision (they say yes or no)

Your role is not to force, but to facilitate clarity and alignment.

This is simply a guided experience that helps someone make a decision.

In fact, I typically teach this: the prospect has often already bought before the call or opt-in.

They're just confirming that you are who they thought you were—and whether they can take advantage of the opportunity at this point in time.

A few funnel examples:

- **Lead magnet funnel:** Ad → Free or low-ticket download → Nurture emails → Offer

- **Webinar funnel:** Ad → Registration → Live or replay webinar → Sales page or call

- **Challenge funnel:** Ad → 3–5 day challenge → Live teaching → Offer pitch

Let each step carry your voice, values, and vision.

Be intentional with your tone and timing.

For sales calls...

I personally allow my spiritual gifts to play a large role in my calls.

I personally allow my spiritual gifts to play a large role in my calls.

I'm a bit "extra" in my businesses.

I heavily qualify each candidate—whether it's for speaking or for consulting/coaching engagements—before any call is booked.

This happens through my booking questions and a thorough screening of profiles and websites.

95% of people cannot book a call with me unless they've either already heard me speak, or made some type of financial commitment beforehand.

Now **by no means** am I saying that you have to do it exactly like I do…

But what I am saying is this: Don't let people waste your time.

Set clear, detailed prequalifiers for any funnel or process that requires your personal attention.

Protect your energy. Protect your calendar. Protect your capacity.

Section 2: Pitching for Engagements

There are many different types of engagements to pitch for. I'll name a few, along with some places you can pitch to right now. But first, something very important: You must be just as prepared to book yourself on your own speaking engagements as you are to get booked on other people's stages.

This means you need to be ready to create your own stages—that is, throw your own events. Depending on budget for ad dollars we encourage our clients to throw 1-5 events and make even more pitches per month. This may seem daunting, but it's quite easy to do once you understand that pitching happens every time you touch any stage... social stages (social media events or talks) included. I created this term to represent any virtual platform or space on social media where individuals showcase their voice, expertise, and offers in real time or pre-recorded.

This is how speakers like me maintain complete financial control and independence over what we earn as speakers. I'll come back to this later, but for now, let me dive into...

How Event Planners Usually Find Speakers:

First... I would say have your speaker sheet/website and a speaker reel(s) available at all times.

Both should be credibility-based and a clear representation of what it will be like to experience you as a speaker and entrepreneur.

This is generally the flow for authorities looking for speakers...

1. Personal Network: "Do I know someone or has someone I trust seen a great speaker recently?"

2. Referrals: They ask close friends or colleagues for suggestions.

3. Extended Network: They post in social communities for speaker referrals.

4. Google Search: If no leads surface, they Google—and book fast based on hype.

Key Insight: If they've reached the Google stage, they are most attracted to an online presence that is very strong—think TEDx talk, press coverage, interviews, 50K+ IG followers.

Keep in mind this is not EVERYTIME.

This is just most times for CONSISTENT engagements in the $10k - $50k+ zone.

However, if your branding and leverage are strong, you can land engagements like this without all the typical credentials.

When you create your own stage and sell products both from the events that book you and your own events, you can consistently walk away with thousands, or even tens of thousands, for your engagements.

I recommend seeking unconventional contact methods to get booked.

Also, find ways to connect with someone who can be a referral or trusted source inside the company.

Skip the generic application links whenever possible.

Go straight to the source through direct channels.

- Send a direct email asking, *"Are you currently accepting speaker applications for your next event? If not you, who should I speak with?"*

Of course, with places like schools or special organizations, there are times when you must go straight through the application link.

Even then, I still recommend adding a personal touch—unless they specifically discourage that.

That personal follow-up can be the difference between getting noticed and getting overlooked

Depending on your network... Peer-to-peer events may be easier to land, but often lack budgets.

If you speak for a lower-fee or nonprofit event, still ask to be compensated.

Your message is valuable. Let them "sow a seed"... even a small honorarium maintains your value.

Email Outreach Tips:

Don't always expect instant replies, a strong brand leaves a lasting impression.

Outreach is a numbers game. Pros are contacting 800+ leads/week. Aim for at least 120/week.

This is why creating your own stage (webinars, workshops, summits) while pitching is essential.

It keeps you visible and in financial control while waiting on booked stages.

Lets talk about Soft and Hard pitches quickly.

You are reaching out to engagements mostly through email and private portals. Simply put you can categorize your pitching formats in these 2 ways :

Soft Pitch - Introduction

○ **Definition:**

A *soft pitch* is an informal or lightly structured approach to getting booked as a speaker. It's typically a personal message (via email, DMs, networking conversations, or referrals) aimed at **introducing yourself** and sparking interest.

○ **Purpose:**

- To initiate a conversation
- To identify the right contact or decision-maker
- To share your general speaking topics and value
- To build rapport without overwhelming with details

○ **Ideal For:**

- Cold or warm leads
- Networking events and mixers
- Event organizers you're newly connected with
- When you're not sure if the event is open to speakers yet

○ **Typical Components:**

- Brief personal intro
- Sometimes one or two signature speaking topics, or a simple mention of your specialty.
- Mention commonality in your beliefs and values
- A sentence or two about your audience results or transformation

- Call to action: "Who do I speak to about being considered as a speaker?" or "Would this be a fit for your audience?"

For an example of this soft pitch please visit **www.thespeakerpreneur.com**

Hard Pitch – *The Formal Proposal*

- ◊ **Definition:**

A *hard pitch* is a formal, structured application to speak. It usually includes a **speaker proposal** or **deck**, goes through a **submission portal**, and targets **clearly open speaking opportunities**.

- ◊ **Purpose:**
  - To apply for a speaking slot officially
  - To compete with other speakers in a formal selection process
  - To showcase your credentials, speaking topics, and value clearly

- ◊ **Ideal For:**
  - Conferences with CFPs (Calls for Proposals)
  - Corporate or high-ticket events
  - Speaking agencies or bureaus
  - Organizations that require deck or speaker submission

- ◊ **Typical Components:**
  - Speaker bio and professional headshot
  - Signature talk titles and descriptions
  - Demo reel or video clips
  - Testimonials or past audience feedback
  - Outcomes or transformation attendees receive
  - Link to media kit or speaker page
  - Submission through a form, portal, or emailed proposal deck

Hard pitches are usually more in depth & tailored to the organization. To see about getting consulting for yours personally… please visit **www.thespeakerpreneur.com**

Here a few overall suggestions:

- Keep your pitch short & direct when applicable—avoid long intros.
- Test email submissions in small batches to track open rates and conversions.
    - Low opens? Your subject line is off.
    - No clicks? The email body isn't converting.
    - No bookings? There's a misalignment or a lack of urgency.

Every outreach email should clearly answer:

1. **What's in it for the reader?**
2. **Why should they trust you?** (Credibility, results, experience)
3. **What do they risk by ignoring you?** (Missed impact, audience dissatisfaction, etc.)

For your speaking engagements and the events you throw…

Only pursue events where:

- The audience is your ideal client or
- They're aligned decision-makers who would benefit from your offer.

And, ensure:

- Your offer fits the room's usual budget.
- You don't waste time on mismatched gigs.

On the next page are a few great places to connect with for engagements.

If you are outside of the US, look for likeness in the organizations near you…

A few great places to connect with for speaking engagements :

- Local Chamber of Commerce

- Non-profit organizations

- Organizations in general within your niche

- Government-funded agencies that serve your community of people

- Eventbrite.com - search for the event organizer and look up on socials for contact and email.

- Facebook events or any other social sites events - search for the event organizer and look up on socials for contact and email.

- Conventions locally and abroad

- Radio Stations & Podcasts

- Contacting speakers who have spoken at your favorite events or similar - utilize them as a referral

- Local Schools & Colleges

- Local Libraries & Book Stores

- Corporations servicing your population already

- Gigsalad

- Gig Master

- SpeakerMatch

- Industry Professional Organizations

- Speaker Hub

- Public Speaking Agencies

- Your Peer Network

- Emailing Your List

- Speaker Bureaus

As you look at this, see what places are in your area and beyond. Write them down here.

_____

_____

_____

_____

_____

_____

_____

_____

_____

_____

_____

_____

_____

_____

_____

_____

_____

_____

_____

_____

_____

_____

_____

If you are throwing your own online events here are some key tools you may want to have in place…

Resources for online training events...

- Paid Advertising Budget
- General Advertising Budget
- Zoom
- Very Strong Computer (minimum 16 GB - iCore 7.. Make sure it's not a Linux)
- Super Strong Internet (if you can hardwire, do so)
- Lighting
- HD Camera
- Dry Erase Board or whiteboard pad
- Dry Erase Markers or stencil
- Canva or PowerPoint presentation maker
- Microphones (1-2 backups)
- iPhone or phone with high pixel quality
- Surge Protected Electric Strips (2 minimum)
- Extension Cords (2 minimum)
- Quiet space with high-quality background in space or HD back screen

Take note of any extra tools you may need or research to be prepared.

_____

_____

_____

_____

Section 3: How to Have a Heart-Centered Sales Call

The next part of this section will be more centered around your sales call with prospects that want to buy your products and personal services.

From the stage you have the ability to sell in many ways.

Some of you may choose to pitch a sale straight from a link or qr code on the screen into a product or service.

Some of you may take your prospect from a link or QR code to a sales call.

Normally, those who go the sales call route are selling high-premium packages or heavily screening prospects.

If that's you...

Sales calls are a powerful way to connect with potential clients and discern whether your offer is a good fit. Here's how to approach them:

Before the call:

- Pray for wisdom and discernment
- Review their application or intake form
- Determine what their main needs are and what your best offers are for them
- Review what their values in business are

In fact, take a look at this basic pre-call prep I generally give my clients when they are new. Some may be repeated from above.

Pre-Call Preparation

30 Minutes Before the Call, Make Sure You Do All of the Following...

- Prepare a quiet room or space where you will not be interrupted.
- Make sure your phone is fully charged. Use headphones so your hands are free for note-taking and expressing yourself.
- Press record on your Zoom or video platform.

- Have a few bullet points nearby to help you stay on track. You should sound focused, not like you're reading a script.

- Place two pre-tested pens and a notepad in front of you.

- Avoid direct screen light on your face; dim your screen or close your laptop to reduce distraction and eye strain.

- Focus on accurately diagnosing their issue, just like a doctor. This is about alignment, not persuasion. Release all attachment to the "yes." Listen deeply and make sure you understand their current situation.

- No eating or drinking during the call. This is a focused, professional space.

- Use the restroom ahead of time, and have a small bottle of water nearby, only in case of emergency.

- Review your client's profile before the call. You may want to reference something personal during the intro to establish a connection.

- Center yourself. Be focused and at peace. Leave the emotions of the day and past calls behind.

- Speak life into this call. Show up aligned with purpose and clarity. This moment matters.

- Have light beaming toward your face so you can be properly lit.

- Have contracts and payment processing systems prepped to be easily and quickly signed.

During the call:

- Create a stress-free, but intentional atmosphere.

- Step in with the intentions for the call so they can understand the process they will be going through today, and set them up knowing that you will pitch at the end if the fit is right.

- Ask questions and have conversation that uncovers their goals, pain points, symptoms, desires, and vision.

- Make sure the prospect not only feels seen and heard, but *is* seen and heard.

- Share how your offer aligns with their needs.

- Speak from certainty and camaraderie, not desperation and selfishness.

- Make the offer with confidence and clarity.

- Make the deal on the call if at all possible, or at least set and secure the deposit. Paperwork should be signed and services set in motion.

- Set the follow-up call if they, for any reason, decline to secure the service at the moment.

- Kill objections throughout the talk and during the pitch.

- Give incentives for joining now.

After the call:

- Send a follow-up email or message even if they have signed on. Have a follow up series ready if they have not.

- If you have not closed yet, for any reason... keep an abundant mindset. Imagine the outcome as well and release the sale.

- Make sure your content topics released in their eye or listening view confirm that they are missing out on something.

Other Notes: You may use many of these tips above to close speaker engagement sales calls, but there are several major differences to note:

Here they are at a glance:

- You're not selling transformation of the event host - to the event host — you're selling audience impact that will benefit the company's agenda.

- In general service calls, the person on the call are the end user.

- In speaking calls, they are the gatekeeper to the audience.

See what aligns and what doesn't and work from there. Stay authentic and honest throughout. You will find yourself falling in perfect alignment from there.

Write down any strengths and weaknesses for your sales call. What can you improve or change for you and your team?

Section 4: The Speaker Contract at it's Core

I would be remiss not to mention making sure that you have a basic, but clear speaker contract is vital. I will condense these factors to get straight to the vital elements of this topic. Having a solid contract and boundaries in place as a speaker and an entrepreneur in whole protects your time, your content, your value, and your reputation. Here's a short but intricate breakdown of the most important notes to keep in mind when it comes to speaker contracts, protecting your content, and spotting red flags before accepting engagements:

Speaker Engagement Contracts: Key Things to Include

1. Clear Scope of Work

- Define what you're being hired for: keynote, workshop, panel, breakout session, etc.

- Include topic, duration, audience size, and expected deliverables (e.g., slides, Q&A).

2. Speaking Fee & Payment Terms

- Clearly state your rate.

- Include deposit details (often 50% upfront).

- Add a payment deadline (e.g., balance due 7 days before event).

- Note preferred payment method and late payment penalties. I am not the biggest fan of checks, but if you must include receive one make sure you have a clear check return fee penalty in the agreement.

3. Travel & Accommodation

- Outline who's covering what: flights, hotel, ground transport, meals.

- Clarify whether it's reimbursed or prepaid.

4. Cancellation Policy

- Define how much notice is required and what's refundable.

- Include a clause for cancellation due to force majeure (acts of God, illness, etc.).

5. Recording & Usage Rights

- Specify whether the host can record your talk (video, audio, livestream).

- Decide if they can use it later for marketing or sales, or if that requires separate permission or compensation.

- Add a clause protecting your intellectual property.

6. Branding & Promotion

- Set guidelines for how your name, title, and likeness will be used in event marketing.

- Request approval rights for promotional materials that use your image or content.

Protecting Your Speaking Content

✓ Copyright Ownership

- Make it clear that your talk, slides, handouts, and exercises are your intellectual property.

- The client is **licensing** your content for one-time use—not owning it.

✓ NDA or Limited Use Clauses

- If you're sharing proprietary business strategies or frameworks, include an NDA or restrict redistribution.

✓ No Reuse Without Permission

- Add a clause that they cannot repurpose, share, or sell your talk without written approval.

✓ Red Flags When Accepting Speaking Engagements

Be cautious if you notice any of the following:

1. Vague Expectations

- They can't clearly articulate the audience, purpose of the event, or what they want from you.

2. No Written Agreement

- If they avoid putting anything in writing or delay sending a contract—it's a liability.

3. "Exposure Only" Offers with No Real Value

- If they promise "great exposure" but have no real audience or plan to promote you, it's likely not worth it.

4. Poor Communication or Last-Minute Scrambling

- Consistently unclear, disorganized, or disrespectful planners often reflect a chaotic experience ahead.

5. No Respect for Boundaries

- They push back on your rate, want free extras, or act entitled to your slides, materials, or time.

6. Host Wants Full Rights to Your Content

- Be wary if they want to own or distribute your talk without limits, especially without compensation.

Bonus Speaker Tip:

- Use your own speaker contract—don't rely only on theirs.

- Consider having a lawyer review your template once and reuse it.

- Use tools like HelloSign, DocuSign, or PDF fillable forms to make it easy for clients to sign.

Section 5: Use Automation Without Losing the Personal Touch

Automation allows you to serve consistently without burnout, but don't let it replace authenticity.

I see this replacement way too often in today's AI-driven society.

There are some things you may not fully want to automate with tech; you may want to automate with a human employee.

You have to feel the client experience to sense what is best.

Automating the wrong way can cost you profit vs making you profit.

I always say, "Use AI, don't let AI use you".

What you can generally automate:

- Lead magnet delivery and consistent email sequences
- Appointment bookings and reminder emails
- Introductory offers and onboarding steps

What generally stays personal in this day and age (because you know a few weeks from now this will change drastically lol):

- Personalized emails or voice notes to hot leads
- Live connection points (lives, certain webinars, Q&As)
- Touchpoints that reflect genuine care

Build a system, but keep your spirit present in the process.

Review what you already have automated or need to automate. How is it for you?

_____

_____

_____

_____

Section 6: Objections Are Opportunities

When someone hesitates, it doesn't mean "no" all the time, sometimes it means "I'm not safe". This person or entity may need clarity or reassurance.

Hesitation is normal.

It's often rooted in fear, uncertainty, or lack of clarity.

Objections are opportunities to educate, support, and realign.

People have several types of objections. A few common ones are :

- Self-Objections
- Family Objections
- Objections About Your Talent
- Time Objections,
- Money Objections

It's your job to get to the root of the objection as best as possible.

You should have an idea of how you will handle objections before you even speak to a prospect because you should know your audience/avatar that well.

This should be practiced.

This helps you handle objections with grace, discernment & use objections as a pivot point to reaffirm value and possibility.

Common objections:

- "I need to pray about it."
- "I don't have the money."
- "I'm not sure if now is the right time."
- "I need to talk it over with my partner."

How to respond:

- Affirm their need to make a wise decision

- Share testimonials or stories of others who had the same fears

- Ask deeper questions to uncover root concerns

- Offer payment plans or lower-tier options if aligned

Here is a map that I give my beginner clients on handling objections. It may help you. I call it the cycle of overcoming objections.

For deeper insight and training on this process, register for our next events at **www.thespeakerpreneur.com.** This way when we are in your area, we can invite you to our next training.

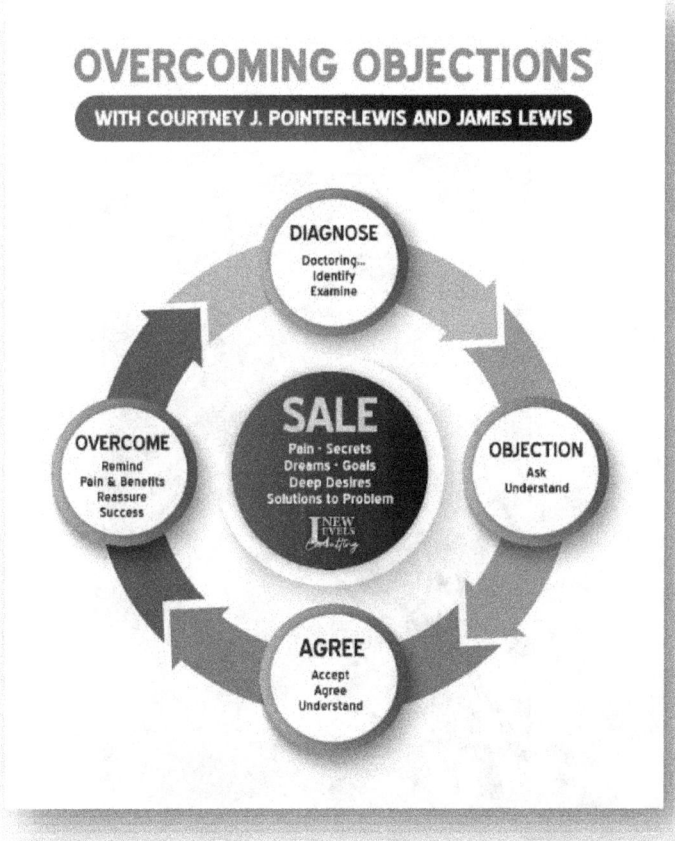

Conclusion: Combine Selling With Faith, Not Fear

Your sales process is an extension of your purpose.

When you lead with love, confidence, and clarity, the right people will say yes and they'll thank you for the transformation they experience.

Trust that what you carry is valuable.

Believe that your offer solves real problems.

Know that selling with integrity honors both your client and your calling.

In the final step, we'll explore how to build backend systems that deliver your offer with excellence and sustain your business with ease.

Now It's Reflection time.

REFLECTION & ACTION TIME

Use this time to reflect over your notes, pray/meditate and make a plan of action from this step accordingly. Use an additional notebook if necessary, add dates and times to carry out the mission.

Goal | (Event that has Occurred in the spirit realm).

What is the specific goal or milestone you're focusing on right now?

_____

_____

_____

Steps Leading to the Goal

Break down the steps you need to take to reach this goal, one by one.

_____

_____

_____

Potential Obstacles

What might get in the way of you completing these steps?

_____

_____

_____

Support System

Who or what can help you overcome these obstacles or keep them manageable?

_____

_____

_____

STEP 12: BACKEND SYSTEMS – DELIVERING WITH EXCELLENCE AND EASE

Introduction: Systems Are a Sign of Strategic Leadership

Your backend systems are not just technical tools— they are reflections of your mindset, preparation, and business maturity.

Many times, they are also an extension of your character, your care, and your calling.

When you deliver your products, coaching, or events with excellence and ease, you embody the order and professionalism that attract success.

Financial independence as a speaker isn't just about making money—it's about maintaining and multiplying it through efficient, scalable systems.

Success isn't just about launching… it's about sustaining.

In these final steps, you'll learn how to build backend systems that help you serve clients consistently, honor their investment, and give you the mental space to operate at a high level.

What systems do you have in place or not have in place that you improve or change? Start to revamp now below and consider what you need.

_____
_____
_____
_____
_____
_____
_____
_____
_____
_____
_____
_____
_____
_____
_____
_____
_____
_____

Section 1: Why Systems Matter for Scale and Sanity

Many new entrepreneurs hit a ceiling because they operate without structure. Strategic systems allow your vision to function even when you step away. At the bare minimum systems help you to:

- Deliver what you promised on time
- Serve clients at a higher level
- Avoid chaos behind the scenes
- Free up time to pray, create, rest, and grow
- Deliver what you promised on time
- Serve clients at a higher level
- Avoid chaos behind the scenes

Reminder: Order creates overflow. Excellence attracts increase. Structure supports freedom. Systems unlock sustainability.

Before we go further let me interject with a quick note, that coincides with what you are about to learn & implement in this section. Let's talk banking and P&L.

P&L: Profit and Loss. This is basically a snapshot of how much money is coming into your business, how much is going out, and what's left over. Some folks also call it an income statement. For now, go ahead and download a basic P&L template. As you move through this section, you'll want to start filling it out and getting comfortable with those numbers.

Now, let's talk about your business bank account. If you're aiming to receive $20K, $50K, or even $100K+ deposits, you need to make sure your bank is ready for that. Not all accounts are built the same, some limit how much cash can clear per day, others might block certain wires or flag international transactions.

Here's what I recommend: Call your bank and ask them straight up... "If I were to receive a $100K deposit, how would that work? Any limits or delays I should know about?" Also ask about wires, purchases, and sending/receiving large amounts of money. Let them walk you through it.

Why does this matter?
Because the more prepared you are to handle big money... the quicker it tends to show up. So don't wait until you're scrambling, get ready now. This is part of shifting into that next-level mindset.

Section 2: Track EVERYTHING. KPI's and their power.

You can't talk about automation and systems without talking about KPIs.

KPIs (Key Performance Indicators) are measurable values that reveal how effectively a person, team, or business is achieving specific objectives. They help track progress toward your goals and guide wise, informed decisions.

Without tracking, you'll never know:

- What systems are working or not working
- What needs to be created
- What should be automated or eliminated

For many of the people I work with, their cash flow, revenue, faith, mental health, and physical health increase by at least 70% once they get serious about KPI tracking.

You are the result of your habits.

Your business is a result of its systems.

Be optimal.

KPIs Will Help You Get:

Specific: Clearly define what's being measured (e.g., "number of new leads per month, number of sleep hours").

Measurable: Quantifiable using data (e.g., sales revenue, conversion rate, physical performance to burnout).

Relevant: Tied directly to business or personal goals.

Time-bound: Measured over a specific time period (e.g., daily, weekly, monthly, quarterly).

Kpi's will Help you…

- Track real progress
- Keep your team focused and accountable
- Make performance transparent and data-driven

- Allow for quick pivots when something isn't working

- Save tons in wasted time and investment dollars

They can be the difference between the highest success and the lowest downfall of the business and yourself.

A few extra & simple examples for speakerpreneurs would be...

- Number of booked speaking engagements per week vs email open/click-through rates

- Total speaking revenue per week

- Lead magnets sold or downloaded per spend or engagement

- Event attendance rate vs show up rate & sign up rate

Note, there are hundreds more KPI's in different areas of life and business.

Dive deeper into this topic with us and with AI at our virtual and in person trainings.

There are so many tools available.

Get VERY serious about tracking your progress and results now vs later.

I'll also give a few coming up.

What KPIs do you currently have in place or need to put in place? What is working for you or not working? Place your notes here...

_____

_____

_____

_____

_____

_____

_____

Section 3 : Basic Core Systems Every Speakerpreneur Business Needs

Note: Many of these can be automated.

Focus on building simple, streamlined systems for:

Speaking/ Entrepreneur Outreach:

- Set up outreach templates for your staff or an automated system to send introductory messages

- Document a process for touch base, so your staff will know what attachments should be sent for inquiries

Client Onboarding:

- Set up automated, yet personalized welcome emails.

- Provide clear next steps and expectations.

- Create a shared folder or portal for materials.

Payment & Checkout Considerations:

- Use Stripe, PayPal or the like to secure payments.

- Offer clear pricing and sensible payment plans. I recommend BNPL as well.

- Automate receipts and confirmations.

- Set up templated invoices.

- Set up pre-filled contracts with questions that contain all necessary values for a speedy response to inquiries.

- If you have closers provide clear templates and instructions as well as training videos for staff to follow your protocol of selling & check out.

Scheduling Considerations:

- Use tools like Calendly or Acuity for booking calls.

- Sync to your calendar and protect your time.

- Include pre-call forms to optimize sessions.

Communication Considerations:

- Choose a primary channel (Slack, Email, Voxer, Telegram, Google Spaces, or anything of the like).

- Set and communicate your availability.

- Maintain consistency in tone and speed of response.

Service Delivery Considerations:

- Set up streamlined processes for staff to provide check-ins and task completions for clientele.

- Provide clear outcomes and structures for client resources to be used for service execution via the same tools from client onboarding.

There are many more, but these are just some of the basics.

Even if you are now playing every role in your business, you should write out and have in place all the systems you use so you can understand what to automate & keep yourself accountable.

Also, in doing so, you can be ready for your team to step in when you obtain one.

Automation systems to cut or save time isn't just AI.

It also includes building a team — and yes, there are even automations for finding the right team.

Make sure to look at many of the Ai systems that allow bots to help with outreach, creating websites, flyers, graphics and the like...

as well as assistance that allows speeches to be created for you to tweak.

I will list some in an upcoming section and more on **www.thespeakerpreneur.com.**

The beauty of business is this:

You're constantly learning how to optimize — and as you do, you naturally start optimizing life better too.

Section 4: Other Tech Tools That Help You Flow

Here are a few popular tech tools you can leverage to support your energy, workflow, and scaling vision. These tools help systemize different areas of your business so you can operate with more ease, excellence, and expansion:

- Kajabi / Thinkific / Teachable – Host and deliver courses, coaching programs, and digital products.

- ConvertKit / Flodesk / Mailchimp – Automate email sequences, segment your list, and nurture leads.

- Google Workspace – Organize docs, spreadsheets, folders, and client notes all in one place.

- Notion / Trello – Track tasks, build systems, map out projects and processes with ease.

- Zoom / Riverside – Run virtual meetings, host workshops, and record content.

- Screencastify / Loom – Create short training videos or personalized screen-recorded messages.

- LastPass – Securely store and autofill passwords across your platforms.

- Eventbrite – Promote, register, and manage in-person or virtual events.

- Upwork: Hire experts for tasks like design, copywriting, admin, or tech.

- Wordtune: An AI-powered assistant to rewrite, enhance, or clarify your writing.

- Descript: Audio and video editing tool that lets you edit media like a text document.

- RocketReach: Find professional contact details for networking or pitching.

- Chatgpt: Create talk titles, outlines, craft proposals, building speaker decks and marketing content faster

- Canva: create stunning visuals for slides, social media, and marketing

I may have a few more tools for speaker engagement outreach that I'll put together for you. Go to **www.thespeakerpreneur.com** and register for the email list.

Choose platforms that feel intuitive, reduce friction, relieve team time, pull and support your goals.

It's not always about saving money, sometimes it's about saving the time that stops the financial increase from happening faster, so be wise… but be open when spending.

What tools do you need to institute right away to help push you forward?

_____

_____

_____

_____

_____

_____

_____

_____

_____

_____

_____

_____

_____

_____

_____

Section 5: Honor the Experience, Not Just the Sale

How you serve after someone says "yes" is just as important as how you attract them.

Your backend is where trust is either built or broken.

Ways to elevate client experience:

- Send a personalized welcome video or note
- Create a smooth, branded onboarding experience
- Check in mid-way through the program(s) to pray, coach, or ask how they're doing
- Celebrate completion with certificates, surprises, or testimonies

A smooth system makes your clients feel seen, supported, and valued.

The experience is the brand.

You won't always be perfect.... Neither will I... but we do the best we can...

And that's amazing enough!

What is your current client experience? What is working and not working? How do you plan to change it today?

_____

_____

_____

_____

_____

_____

_____

_____

Section 6: Protect Your Time and Mental Space

As you may have noticed earlier when we talked about KPIs—systems aren't just for clients... they're also for you.

You've probably heard the phrase, "You can't pour from an empty vessel."

It's repeated often, but it's not true...

The truth is... you can.

The issue is if you continue to pour from an empty vessel, you'll still pour... but what you give will be fragments, fumes, and burnout disguised as generosity.

Eventually, your presence becomes a performance, your joy becomes duty, and your impact begins to suffer.

You won't stop giving... you'll just give from depletion instead of overflow.

That's why rest, refilling, and soul-care aren't luxuries... they're leadership strategies.

Your vessel matters.

Keep it full. Then give freely from the overflow.

Many entrepreneurs silently battle burnout, illness, and emotional overload—some to the point of breakdown. Sadly, the suicide rate among entrepreneurs is high.

True, financially independent and fulfilled speakerpreneurs understand:

All areas of health must be prioritized, not just financial health. So get outside help in all areas! Hire professionals in EVERY area of your needs to lessen the blows.

That's why it's critical to apply the same mindset you use for automating business tasks and serving your clients, to your own well-being.

Use:

- Automation
- SOPs (Standard Operating Procedures)
- Boundaries

...not just to run your business, but to guard your energy, mental peace, and joy.

Note: In business, an SOP (Standard Operating Procedure) is a step-by-step written document that outlines how to perform a specific task or process consistently and efficiently. It ensures clarity, streamlines delegation, and protects both your brand and time by making your operations repeatable and scalable.

The same mentality can be applied to life.

Ask:

- What do I keep doing manually that can be automated?
- What/who would make my delivery process more peaceful?
- Where can I simplify or outsource without compromising my voice?

If you're a person of faith like myself... you understand that faith doesn't cancel planning... it empowers it.

For some of you, food prep is vital. A housekeeper, even just twice a month, can make a huge difference. Having someone wash clothes for you might be the game-changer you didn't realize you needed.

An alarm set for a monthly therapy session—on autopilot—could be the difference between a breakdown and a full shutdown of life and business.

Don't neglect the small changes.

Making those "small" adjustments are huge and they add up. This is also true for the small changes not instituted.

From the previous questions, there may be a lot going through your mind. Feel free to bring them up here.

_____

_____

_____

_____

_____

Conclusion: Build to Last, Not Just to Launch

You've come through an entire transformation journey—from vision to voice, to offer, to brand, to systems.

Your backend isn't an afterthought... it's a reflection of your maturity and readiness for more.

When you deliver in healthy order, with care, clarity, and consistency, you're preparing for sustainable growth.

You're honoring the people God sends and preparing for the increase he has planned.

Stay faithful.

Stay organized.

Stay open to the new.

Your journey as a Speakerpreneur is just beginning and now you have the systems to support the weight of your purpose.

Now It's Reflection time.

Here's some extra space to create a plan of action.

_____

_____

_____

_____

_____

_____

_____

_____

_____

REFLECTION & ACTION TIME

Use this time to reflect over your notes, pray/meditate and make a plan of action from this step accordingly. Use an additional notebook if necessary, add dates and times to carry out the mission.

Goal | (Event that has Occurred in the spirit realm).

What is the specific goal or milestone you're focusing on right now?

_____

_____

_____

Steps Leading to the Goal

Break down the steps you need to take to reach this goal, one by one.

_____

_____

_____

Potential Obstacles

What might get in the way of you completing these steps?

_____

_____

_____

Support System

Who or what can help you overcome these obstacles or keep them manageable?

_____

_____

_____

PUTTING IT ALL TOGETHER

So here we are...

These steps are simple, but life-changing. Keep the answers to these questions in an organized place according to each step. You will need them all.

Business is a journey and you are responsible for every bit of it. My goal has been to make finding the answers inside that process much easier for you.

It's not your coach's responsibility, your consultant's responsibility, your mentor's or anyone else's responsibility to guarantee your success...

It's not even God's... because He has already given you the power to obtain wealth (Deuteronomy 8:18).

It's on you to utilize your tools now.

AND... You got this!

I still want to help you on that path though... the same way I wanted help, but couldn't always find it.

These 12 powerful steps are the mastery that you will immerse yourself in further to create wealth and financial independence in your speakerpreneur journey and even in your life.

Use this mini guide as a manual that you will continue to go back to as you are learning from myself and your other mentors.

Buy one of these guides for your friend or family member so you can create wealth together!

You will start to research and dig deeper into some of the elements I mention here, which is the point... and questions will arise.

If needed, bring me to your church or small group... If I'm available my team will do their very best to accommodate or find an event near you that we are hosting.

We generally have private training events all over the world year-round for you to stay in momentum and get further help.

We also have private mentorship programs to give you intensive accountability and speed. Don't *delay* your purpose any longer.

Join our communities for accountability.

Go to **www.thespeakerpreneur.com.**

Finally...

Don't sleep on your calling.

Your purpose is depending on you…

And you were built for this!

Let me be the first to congratulate you in advance on your full-time financial independence through Speakerpreneurship!

May God continually bless you and prosper you in every area.

Your coach/mentor,

Minister Courtney J.

ABOUT THE AUTHOR

Courtney J. Pointer-Lewis is a visionary minister, speaker & coach specializing in sales, marketing, speaking and marketplace ministry.

As one of the only known operating African American, faith based female speaker/business coaches with a wealth of experience across 30 to 60+ niches at this time... Courtney has consulted thousands of speakers and businesses from new to high 6 & 7 figure ranges; guiding them to scale, become global impactors & tap into their supernatural money-making abilities.

Having clientele features on Essence Fest, Forbes, Ted X, NBA, Miss America Pageants, Women's Health Magazine, Sirius XM and many more...

She is known to have speakers placed on between 10 - 120 paid stages yearly & to quadruple sales for businesses in just under 3 months.

As the CEO of New Levels Consulting, she is redefining how faith-driven professionals and companies overall achieve ultimate success in their respective fields.

To book Minister Courtney J. for your next event, or inquire about mentorship email: <u>courtneyjplewispress@gmail.com</u>

www.ingramcontent.com/pod-product-compliance
Lightning Source LLC
Chambersburg PA
CBHW071501150426
43191CB00009B/1397